Arkansas Poetry Award Series

News from Where I Live

POEMS BY

Martin Lammon

The University of Arkansas Press
Fayetteville   1998

02   01   00   99   98   5   4   3   2   1

Designed by Alice Gail Carter

☺   The paper used in this publication meets the mini-
mum requirements of the American National Standard
for Permanence of Paper for Printed Library Materials
Z39.48-1984.

LIBRARY OF CONGRESS CATALOGING-IN-PUBLICATION DATA

Lammon, Martin, 1958–
     News from where I live : poems / by Martin Lammon.
       p.   cm.
     ISBN 1-55728-507-1 (cloth : alk. paper). —
     ISBN 1-55728-508-X (pbk. : alk. paper)
     I. Title
PS3562.A46434N48   1998
811'.54—dc21   97-39769
                                         CIP

For my mother, for stories she tells me
For my father, for stories he keeps to himself

ACKNOWLEDGMENTS

I would like to thank the following journals in which poems or
original versions of poems were first published:

Chariton Review	"Naming Day"
	"The Secret of Saturday Morning"
Gettysburg Review	"The Emperor's Dog Finds the Way Home"
	"How I Learned to Count"
	"Love in Slow Motion"
	"What We Feel in Our Bones"
Midwest Quarterly	"Valley Falls"
Mississippi Valley Review	"When They Are Not Alone"
New Virginia Review	"A Japanese Woman Confides in Me and Speaks of Heaven"
Nimrod	"The Men of Springtime"
	"Three Poems for One Traveler"
	"Nearing Sixty, a Man Declares Himself a Romantic" Selected by W. S. Merwin for a 1997 *Nimrod*/Hardman Pablo Neruda Prize in Poetry.
Ploughshares	"Stories a Man Keeps to Himself"
Raystown Review	"In the Church of Saint Stephen"
Southern Poetry Review	"Where the Children Go"
West Branch	"Like New Gods, Two Japanese Women Guide My Hands"
	"Three Short Clay Poems":
	"The Anagama Kiln"
	"A Clay Bowl"
	"What We Have in Common"

I also wish to acknowledge the West Virginia Commission on the
Arts for a 1994 fellowship in poetry that provided support during
the completion of this work.

CONTENTS

III.   *The Way Back*

I promised to show you a map you say but this is a mural
then yes let it be   these are small distinctions
where do we see it from is the question

—Adrienne Rich, "An Atlas of the Difficult World"

Chia-Shun laughs also,
and closes the book, and says,
"When I see these pictures, when I remember these things"
—he looks like a boy, wild and pink with excitement—
"I want to live two hundred years!"

—Donald Hall, "Photographs of China"

I. *Crazy for Paradise*

NEWS FROM WHERE I LIVE

After reading Associated Press reports, Good Friday, 1991

In Cutad, north of Manilla, six men
are nailed to crosses in a rice field.
A crucified fish vendor weeps
because his mother was sick
then well again.
                    In the Colosseum, the Pope
carries a five-foot cross. Beneath
the Roman moon he leads a torchlight
procession, the long walk of Jesus to Calvary.

And in Jerusalem, Christians follow
the *Via Dolorosa*. Each carries a cross.
John Moore of Maryland walks beside
fifteen Arabian priests in black robes.
"You feel you have to whisper," he says.

Where I live the *Altoona Mirror* publishes
two photographs on the front page:

In the first, Tanya Glass, age nine, poses
like a tent revival evangelist,
and in her small hands the *Holy Bible*
opens like black wings; in the other photo
the girl spreads her arms as if she will fly
off the page. She is showing the way
Jesus (Jason McCauley, age seven) should suspend himself
on the cross he props on his back. What he carries
is a long forked stick, the kind a prospector
might cut for a rod to divine where water hides.

In Altoona, boys and girls practice for posterity
at birthday parties and the Bavarian Club Octoberfest.
Proud mothers and fathers preserve snapshots
in worn shoe boxes salvaged from Christmas.

Years from now, an old woman will shuffle
photographs stacked high as a pinochle deck,
let her finger pause on a girl's blurred face—
                    heal herself a little.

IN THE CHURCH OF SAINT STEPHEN

You just never know what people will say. In Ebensburg,
Pennsylvania, in the Laurel Lounge, a woman tells me
she is lucky, how her father
never laid a hand on her; how in Cambria County
a girl is thankful if her father ignores her.

So we dance all Saturday night, hold on
to each other, and let ourselves go
to hell, and go happily
out into the dark parking lot. She says she can't
go home with a married man, couldn't live with herself
Sunday morning.

                 In the Church of Saint Stephen,
pews cut from Laurel Highland pine will not warp.
Joints and iron buckles will last, might as well
say so, forever. Old coal men who built this church
let their women shave them, their jaws and chins, gentle
as women can. Mines had turned skin raw. The sons of men
who built this church liquor each other up
with schnapps while their wives scheme ways to keep them
from coming home drunk and eager to work out their women
in bed, or hard against the kitchen floor.

In the Church of Saint Stephen, a father's palm clamps
around the pew's curved seat, his hand
so close to his daughter's
she thinks he might take hold,

a man I imagine on the steps of Saint Stephen,
finally articulate:

> *If I never took money from my kids' hands*
> *for liquor nor tobacco,*

if I never took skin off their bodies
when I slapped my belt against them naked,
if I never took my daughter down
into the cellar weeping,
I got more right to heaven than you
that never put up a church, nor bloodied
socks frozen to your feet in winter.

Sober or drunk, I'd hold my own father if I could
to one promise. I'd lean down close, my ear
to his lips. He'd whisper, and then I'd sit down
beside his bed, wait for him
to die, his hand rigid
in mine, the good death I want for him. For me.

At the Church of Saint Stephen, I could sit beside
that woman I knew, hold her hand,
repeat for her my father's last three words,

a common phrase we'd hold him to.

STORIES A MOTHER COULD TELL

The stories I could tell you, how your father proposed
that quiet night in April, 1956, warmest planting
anyone remembered. Your father drove
me home that night, swerved off the road
where tractors flattened a path
between cornfields. That spring, the land
plowed over, the soil was so black
farmers in Fulton County swore
come summer even fence posts might sprout.

Your father and I parked, quiet a long time—listened
to crickets, the radio. My bare legs itched. He told me to open
the glove box, and I found the ring he'd hidden there.
It was my eighteenth birthday.

How I wanted
out of my father's house, how I loved your father
that night, his kisses so deep I was dizzy, his hand
on my knee, on my thigh.

How in a '48 Ford I wanted all of him.

Now I live in a town I'd never
heard of when I was a girl. Not much anymore
dazzles a woman my age. I sing in the church
choir, and teach children
whose fathers played little league baseball with you, whose mothers
whispered about boys they'd marry—maybe even giggled
your name. Lord, that was twenty-five years ago.

But in that world I used to live in,
a mother held her weeping son, hugged
his heaving shoulders because she knew how,
soon, he would not let her touch him this way.

The stories I might tell you
I could not speak out loud. How one night your father
wanted all of me, how I knew
what he wanted, and what to do.

When you lie down with a woman, curtains closed, your face
so near she feels you breathing, I know what she feels
is the story a woman keeps to herself.

LOVE IN SLOW MOTION

Today we are watching a movie. Mrs. Daniels
teaches us. Behind our backs her voice
fills the room the way God must sound
inside a priest's head. "You see,
children," she tells us, "it grows too slowly
for the naked eye, this miracle
science shows us." Here is what we see: a jittery
seed, its skin unpeeling, root and stem
wedging through dirt; leaves and petals
unfurling and blooming. I wonder
if the girl beside me notices the way I watch
her, how I want to kiss her cheek, how I worry
she will know what I am thinking.

In the dark room, we lean
our elbows against carved wooden
desks, wobbly and stained. Others
have chiseled their initials here. The girl who sits
beside me, the one
I'd pass notes to if she loved me, yawns
and picks up her pencil. She digs the point into deep
grooves and daydreams about a boy who would love her
enough to leave letters dug into soft wood.

In my science book there is a note card
pasted inside the back
cover. All our names are listed here, all of us
this book has belonged to. In 1958, the year I was born,
a girl took the book to bed. She would have worn
nail polish and lipstick. She would have read how

the food chain and photosynthesis
converge, how every animal metabolizes oxygen,
how the engines of leaves churn
sunlight and carbon dioxide into what we breathe.

How everything is invisible, incremental, and patient.

WHAT A BOY MIGHT HAVE WRITTEN
BEFORE HIS SUICIDE

When my hand follows the curve of her hip
I know how our teacher's formula fails,
how only the body explains
what's beautiful in this world. My bass guitar
thumps inside my chest, so deep I think fingers
pluck between my ribs. First period choir
is God's voice, soprano, alto, baritone, and tenor
the filaments that weave our chorus
together. When her mouth closes over mine,
I know what I know.

              My love,
my fingertips burn where I touch your thigh.
When you lie beside me under stars, each needlepoint
of light pricks my bare arms. I remember once
a priest explained how a boy's eyes would go blind
if he stared into the face of God, and how I should not
be so curious. Once, my mother warned me
to look away from the sun's eclipse, said my eyes would
sizzle like bacon frying, only I wouldn't know
until too late. How can I face you

my love? Sometimes if I lie down
in the basement, if I close my eyes
in that dark place, I can almost feel nothing
but cold cement damp against my skin.

I am on fire
all the time. Whether this is hell or heaven
I cannot live here. I cannot breathe
this air. I cannot go barefooted. I cannot hold

my hands over my ears forever. This world is not
safe. But you are
so deep inside me that I am not afraid
I might only be crazy.

Is there a prayer for me? Keep it
for another—whisper those holy words
into his ear. I'll be there. I promise.
He will understand if I listen.

SIGN LANGUAGE

The woman he loves holds his hand.
With her fingers
she spells "water," "mother,"
"I love you," and he learns
how Annie Sullivan
taught Helen the body's words
for the cool river
in July, for the soft shoulder
where daughter lay her head.

The woman he loves holds
his hand. She leans
her head down to kiss
each knuckle, the curve
between thumb and forefinger.

After a long rain cleans the air
and the night sky is open and cold, the shiver
along his neck when he looks up
and loses himself looking at stars
is the body's sentence: *I want to believe.*

Or, the muscular heart's:
I am afraid
I want you more than this body
can withstand the pressure
of its blood.

WHEN THEY ARE NOT ALONE

Yes, right now
he wants to love her
in his worn
doctor's chair, where
long nights alone
he hunches
and types.

Tonight, they are
not alone
and he would
love her, right now,
just where she is
sitting, typing
her late report due
so early next
morning.

How he wants
to leave his body
out of this
work they must do

but the chair
swivels
full circle
on its oiled screw
and tilts
just far enough
instinct
seizes them. They

fall back
into the heart's
pulse, the shudder

they cannot resist when
their bodies are falling
into that deep
well of gravity
and longing.

STORIES A MAN KEEPS TO HIMSELF

. . . for it seemed to me that everybody ought
to know about it, but I was afraid to tell, because
I knew that nobody would believe me . . . .

—FROM *Black Elk Speaks*

It's a strange night here in West Virginia, warm
for November, one last thunderstorm before winter
comes on. Rain rattles against metal
awning, as if Oglala drummers surrounded
my house. They pound hollow bones against skinned
logs. Perhaps long thigh-bones of Wasichu
killed last summer, or buffalo slaughtered long ago
after a boy's first hunt.

                    This is the way I think these days.
When I read what Black Elk dreams, and what he remembers,
I know something creeps into me that keeps me awake at night
and that I take with me when I sleep. How a Sioux man
falls in love with a woman and follows her even though
she will not talk to him. He hides in the bush near
the river where she bathes or washes clothes. He waits
for hours just so he can be alone with her and talk about love.
He offers a dozen ponies he does not have, or a hundred,
because he knows he will borrow or steal them if he has to,
just so he can love her forever.

                    I know I have no right
to that man's life, and that Black Elk did not live
or die so that I might make this poem. I am Wasichu, I live
in a box. My music is not his music, I have no fire, and I
could not kill a man even if I hated him. I'd be the first
to die in a fight, or hunting buffalo for three days in deep snow.

But there are stories I can't get rid of, so many lives
crowded inside me, not in my head
so much, but in my chest, where the Greeks found
the soul—*pneuma* they called it; "pneumonia" what we call
the sickness that steals our breath—and it is a kind of sickness
that Black Elk felt when he lay in fever for twelve days
and journeyed with his grandfathers, and that I feel
in the wing-bones of my hips the day after
I make love to a woman I'd give
anything to have beside me now. A hundred
nimble ponies.

But tonight there's just this strange rain
beating on my roof. The only other sound is moths
hurling their bodies against the porch light, as if lost
spirits possessed them, crazy for paradise.

THE SECRET OF SATURDAY MORNING

It is a simple recipe, she says,
so I peek into her bowl
and, yes, even I can see
there is butter, flour, a little sugar,
and raisins. Do you like them?
she asks, and I know she means
the raisins, so I say
yes, but what I mean is

how beautiful you are
on a Saturday morning,
stirring a spoon slowly;
how it is the way your hand
turns and rolls, devoted to this
simple task, baking muffins
with raisins for us, and how
sweet I know they will taste,

but what I say is, yes,
and again, a little softer, yes.

VALLEY FALLS

All morning, rain soaks the small river.
Water gushes over mossy rocks. For a moment
you think you might dance across
barefoot and fearless.

Old branches snap from trees and are swept away.
Old roots tangle in the bank's loose soil. You think
you might dig your fingers into this mud, hold
hands with a love you've waited for
since before you were born. The river

rumbles toward the falls. Blood
hurtles through the valves of your heart

and you think you could find a new life
inside the source of all falling water.

THE MEN OF SPRINGTIME

Ilira *is the fear that accompanies awe;* kappia *is fear*
in the face of unpredictable violence. Watching a polar
bear—ilira. *Having to cross thin sea ice*—kappia.

—BARRY LOPEZ, *Arctic Dreams*

One hundred seventy years ago, European whalers
hunted *Balaena mysticetus*
in Pond's Bay, north of Baffin Island. The Greenland
right whale, or Bowhead, was slow; it floated
when killed; pound for pound, its bone and oil
made men rich. It was *the*
whale, the *right* whale, to hunt, but not easy
to kill. Whalers slaughtered thousands. The native
Tununirmiut called these strangers
"the men of springtime." By the summer of 1832
all the local villages were silent. The Eskimo
had died during the winter from diptheria and smallpox.

Yaks the whalers called them.

~~~~~~

Summer in West Virginia, the year I turn
thirty-five, my fears are common:

that I have lived for nothing more
than a small house I do not own;
that I shall die before I've written a poem
my whole life depends on;
that a woman I love will not speak to me.

Last March, when a blizzard
heaped snow against my windowsill, when I was
alone, when the evening air
was phosphorescent, I could not sit still.

All I could do was pace, shake, weep. I listened
to the white wind. A wave of snow
banked across my road, as if an arctic ocean
would swell over my house, swallow me whole.

~~~~~~~

The men of springtime were seized by glaciers cracking, falling
like mountains into the sea; by white belukha whales
haunting like ghosts the keels of their ships; by *water
burning like manganese in the evening sun.* Many whalers
died. The Eskimo had lived
a thousand years in this place, had learned
words for *the fear that accompanies awe,
fear in the face of unpredictable violence.*

Ilira. Kappia. I look for words that will name
the fears my body knows, what only my body
can translate faithfully: How an unexpected
blizzard seizes me, or a woman's blue eyes—
the apparition of her face adrift in falling snow.

WHAT WE FEEL IN OUR BONES

One night a woman tells me, "I wouldn't have the courage
to kill myself, or the instinct." Her fingers
stroke the bones that wrap around her eyes.
She rubs the hollows between bones.

I remember Senior Anatomy, the cat's
skeleton, how Mr. Mitchell traced his finger along
lumbar and thoracic vertebrae up to where the medulla
oblongata would attach to the neck's stem. The skull
looked to me like a girl's fist, and I wanted
to hold it in my hands, my thumbs laid against
each zygomatic arch—as if cheekbones might be
a portal to a new kind of heaven where
infinitesimal gods plotted inside a cat's head.

Where do you scribble an answer like that on the teacher's
quiz? What do you say to a woman
who rubs her eyes as if she'd stared too long at the sun,
or down, where new snow glitters
like god-fire? You say nothing. This is the way
love ends, the way your hands go numb,
then toes, the way an old man
feels in his bones there's no one
who will rouse him from his bed.

II. *The Way to the New World*

THE SECRET OF THE PLATYPUS

What could this curious mélange be,
beyond a divine test of faith and patience?

—STEPHEN JAY GOULD, *"To Be a Platypus"*

Outside my window, a hill
rises, the same
as every morning this summer.
I sit in my chair and read Gould's argument
for the marvelous platypus, whose species
dull biologists have relegated
to a lesser rank within *Mammalia*,
or I write a new poem
about mothers or fathers, cows
or trout. I lift up my head to look at the hill,
how it slopes above our neighborhood's
houses. I do not know how high
but steeper and wilder, I think, than I
could climb. I watch the dawn
fog dissolve into the haze of August.

The platypus swims across the river, lays
eggs in the mud, and does not love my poem.
The hill does not need me
wedging my boot against some tender
root. The shrub has its own life. One leaf
strains for a little sunlight. So what if I cannot
witness the way leaves work? I know they stretch and curl
for one day's glory all their own, even if I don't
know how. And if I did sink my boot into mud
where no one had ever walked before, no photographer
or archeologist would celebrate that I had
climbed this hill. The maple, if it noticed me at all,

would shrug and endure my hug around its trunk, a man's
simple panic against gravity.

This morning, I sit in my chair
and read about the platypus, whose strange wet fur
glistens in the moonlight, or I write a poem about a beautiful
woman. There are so many lives whose secrets
do not belong to me, lives beside my own
whose secrets are worth loving.

A JAPANESE WOMAN CONFIDES IN ME AND SPEAKS OF HEAVEN

Two hours by car outside Tokyo, where wind
ripples through rice fields, where silhouettes of cows
float across the ridge at dusk, Grandfather's house
is rubble now. In the backyard there was once a wooden shed
he hammered together before the war when he was just twenty-two.
Inside the shed, he'd bathe in a giant iron pot.

As a girl, I'd listen to crickets when,
half behind the horizon, the sun turned the sky red.
The breeze was cool against my skin. Inside the house
I'd tuck myself under Grandmother's arm and beg for a bath.
She'd smile and walk out to the backyard for firewood.
In half an hour she'd return, the water ready, and I'd see her face
smudged where she wiped her cheek hot from the fire.

I'd walk outside barefoot on the damp grass
to Grandfather's wooden shed, whose boards were swollen
and split by summer heat and winter snows.
I'd tug open the door and there it was, huge and black.
The iron pot, rusted here and there,
looked like a giant injured beetle crouching
above a fire's embers. All alone,
I'd undress, fold my clothes over a chair,
then rinse my body with cool water in the sink.

If you bathe in an iron pot, you must squat
on a wooden plank wedged into the curved bottom
or the metal will burn you; if you never soaked
in a giant iron pot, or watched the autumn stars
through crevices in a thatched roof, you cannot know
why I sang so loudly. A lady of the neighborhood cried,

"Stop singing such a clumsy song!" I am embarrassed
to tell you, I broke wind in the hot water, bubbles gurgling up to my chin.

They are dead now, Grandfather and Grandmother, but I tell you
Heaven is a giant iron pot
where old men and women soak and sing
and are young again. There's water enough
that I could join them. I am not afraid of dying.
Heaven is curved, and deep enough to bathe in.

LIKE NEW GODS, TWO JAPANESE WOMEN
GUIDE MY HANDS

Their fingers flutter
like feathers, like a boy's prayers.
Crane's wings lift and wave.

They hand me paper,
square wafer I twist and crease—
where is calm water

for the crane I make?
I pucker and blow on wings,
a Japanese wind

inhabits me here,
what claim have I on the air?
New gods are welcome

in my house and sit
at the head of my table.
Let us feast and share

our oldest stories:
a paper crane soars at night—
why not? Two women

guide my hands, we love
the creatures our fingers shape.
The old prayers, we keep:

"Very beautiful,"
they say, and *Hai,* I say yes—
human holy words.

FROM WEST VIRGINIA, A FURTHER
WESTWARD JOURNEY

A woman tells me
how sometimes she feels so small
on a starry night.

We walk together,
laugh—now and then I turn
my head, and she smiles

the way I love. She
is shivering. The night is cold.
I want to tell her:

I will make a fire
for us from driftwood we find,
then lie down beside you

on the sand, look up
and say nothing, just listen
to Pacific waves.

She tells me again
how the stars are hard to see
in Japan—that place

where she used to live,
so far away now, so close.
She says, "I want to

"show you Kyoto,"
and I want her to teach me
the secrets she knows,

shrines that are sacred
to millions of wanderers,
how to eat noodles

and rice, how to give
your shoulder to a stranger
on a crowded bus.

When I hold her close
to me, her body opens
a world that is not

small, but hard to find.
The fire burns low. Shadows.
"I want to see you,"

she says, after we
make love. In the dark, we lay
new wood on the fire.

Three Poems for One Traveler

tabibito to
wa ga na yobaren
hatsushigure

—BASHŌ

I .

Blue Hole Cave, my guide tells me,
is for beginners. He points to a wedge
between rocks, tells me this is the cave's
mouth—and I believe him. You cannot
walk upright
through the opening. You lie back, slide
your legs through, scoot
down a small, dark gullet. My guide
explains how caves breathe, the science
of pressure and temperature,
of equilibrium. I do not tell him
how I hear a strange
sigh, as if a man were in
love or had just finished
a good supper of rice
and fish. I decide for myself
the cave's name is
a man's, and that I can
almost pronounce his name.

2 .

There are no vowels in ancient
Egyptian writing—those sounds
were made by breath, sacred
in that old tongue. So when we write
in English letters *hekau*
we diminish
ourselves. We cannot imagine
a language of braided rope, hands
lifted up in praise, a bound
scroll, or remember how these hieroglyphs
inspire our translation: *Words of power.*
We are dispossessed
of the heart's muscle, of hands
that could stretch up to heaven, of hoarse
windpipe. We say *spiritus*, or how the hieroglyphs
inspire us, but we are not afraid enough
of God's breath, the *hex*
that animates our lungs
when love seizes us.

3 ·

Traveler, Bashō asks
to be called, *when winter's first showers*
change to snow. There is so much
I have to learn, so much
my body knows.
My teachers help me
laugh again
and tremble
the way a man in love
laughs and sighs
in the same breath. How did this happen,
that I am in love for the first time
with a woman, and not
the idea of a woman?

One long breath
is enough for me
to recite the old *hokku* for all of us
travelers: *fallen leaves,*
we do not know
when the wind will take us.

Cafe Negro at Soda Pinini

THE MAN WINSTON McCLOUD, HE KNOW

The Way Lizard Breathes

Lizard's tail twitches, tests the air.
Lizard's tongue tastes gnat's nearness.
Lizard's ribs squeeze in and out,
rapid as hummingbird's wings.

Magical Realism in Cahuita, Costa Rica

"Jesus Lizard," they say here.
Basilicus run
fast. He skim over water.

Realism Solo

"Lizards, what do you call them?"
I ask. Winston McCloud
say, "We call dem lizards."

WATER COCONUT KNOW WHAT COMING

Pipa's branch look like bird's wing—
palm leaf, like many feathers.
When air ruffle, just two leaves
twitter. The rest are still.
"Rogue breezes," crazy gringa tell me.

ONE LANGUAGE

In Spanish, say: *ma-CHE-te*.
Again: mah-CHAY-tay.

Machete open pipa,
or swipe yard's long grass.

Machete make wide arc
like sun in the sky.

No *chistes* today. No jokes.

THIS IS THE WAY HE SPEAK

Morning, man with machete
cut tall grass. All day
he sweep blade side to side.

This is the way he work. Man
with long stick knock down
oranges. This is the way

he eat and drink when sun is
high and hot. His bike
lean beside mossy pipa.

When sun go down, man pedal
slow on muddy road.
This is the way he get home.

ALL THE NAMES I DO NOT KNOW

Flora, Fauna, Frog

Bananas ripening here,
green going to yellow—
how *rana* learned its name.

Dendrobatid

Long name
for thumb-sized, shiny
rana. Almost missed you
hidden among leaves
close to muddy path.

Maybe Talamanca coast
Cabécar men, or
KéköLdi tip arrows
with rana's poison.
I don't know. Many old ways

are lost here, same as back home.
But dendrobatid
is not lost. Its small body
knows how shocking green
can be, like no Ohio frog.

THE FIRST THREE NAMES OF RAIN

Are not my father's spitter, his name for when
the lake's bluegill love best to nibble; nor clever holler
preacher's gullybuster, coal miner's altar call; nor even
come bedtime, your sweet grandmother's angel's tears.

Morning, my love and I learn how rain lures us
back to bed, how rainfall's rhythm beats
against palm branch, metal roof, banana's
leafy elephant ears. We sink beneath a gravity of rain.

Afternoon, rain soaks grass and wood, leaf
and juice maker. Rain muddies the slim path
in the forest, swells *gambas*, those spiral roots that twist
like fingers out of damp soil, merge, become the *Chonta* tree.

At night, before rain reaches your house,
you hear ocean and storm roar together, those two great waters,
and wait for rain to sweep over beach and tall *cocos*. Today,
or *mañana*, just wait: Maybe you learn the first three names of rain.

Three Short Clay Poems

THE ANAGAMA KILN

There is a difference. In America
most clay bakes in gas or electric
brick kilns, fires faithful
to knobs and valves. The Japanese Anagama

is a wood-burner, looks like a bunker
a crazy man built against angry gods,
or a giant mud dauber's nest. Every hour
day and night, men and women trade shifts,
stoke the kiln, pile on split logs,
scrap wood. The watchers peer inside,
gauge heat, and learn how fickle
fire is. In the Anagama a hundred pots,
plates, cups, and shapes—fish head,
turtle shell, dragon coil—blister and crack
or harden like fossils wedged in old mud.

At night, anxious potters whisper in the dark
glow of fire they are faithful to.

A CLAY BOWL

In Japan, a Master's hands
sink into wet clay which spins
out into a bowl on the potter's wheel,
thumbs hollowing out the place
where rice will steam, or flowers
gather into one new fragrance
then wilt and spoil
as flowers must do. In Japan

a Master's clay bowl, fired and glazed
in the Anagama kiln, is beautiful
enough to serve supper in, to hold
what withers under the sun.

WHAT WE HAVE IN COMMON

In the house I grew up in, my mother
surprises us when she mixes
her good Wedgwood dishes—a wedding gift
twenty summers old—with the cracked
plates stacked recklessly in her cupboard.

My mother tells me how, on her father's farm,
she shimmied on her knees in the baked Ohio dirt
and snipped green beans from the vine
for ten cents a row, and how
she dreamed of china patterns, delicate
coffee cups she would pose
behind glass panes of a cherry oak
cabinet. Older now, she gives in

to common sense, in America
the place where wealth
and poverty may be forged
in fiery fables we learn to spin
in the flickering rhythm of summer's heat
as if pedaling the treadle of the potter's wheel.

III. *The Way Back*

NAMING DAY

Each of us holds on to what we have
lost, our first language, the one
we were born with, loose
and rattling somewhere inside us.

Years ago, my grandfather's supper prayer
was a mumble, only his *Amen*
sounded safe. We drank *millich*
from Sterling's Dairy—*scheiss,* he'd mutter
if his daughter sassed him.

All these years
I did not understand my mother's
first name: *Licht-en-wald,*
a clearing in the woods.

One night I dreamed
I was speaking German.
I opened my eyes
and I knew
I'd understood every word.

Grandfather hadn't been dead long. And me?
I turned out the lights, went back
to sleep. That morning, I woke up
to crying, the old smell of milk.

WHERE THE CHILDREN GO

Children toddle, swoop, and holler
in the yard next to mine. I cannot
guess what they are playing, their games
no more familiar
than the first time I balanced a bicycle, or the first
time I made love, and nerves fluttered.
One girl wanders away from her friends, stares
as if she sees
the woman she will become.

A willow tree or mulberry bush revives the old farm
where my great-grandfather
sits in the rocker on his porch, watches
the tiny cousins play tag among
shrubs and weeping willows.
He leans forward and calls:

kommenkinder, kommenkinder.

He is enormous, red-faced. A bald scalp
slopes down his forehead. Spotted and hairy
hands reach out to me. The cuffs
of his sleeves recede halfway to his elbows.

When I was three years old, my mother wanted me
to look this man in the eyes. They were
the color of roots dug out of loose soil.

Somewhere in a country I do not know, near
the Volga River, they tell me
there's a cemetery this man's mother is buried in,

where a stone cross marks her grave. And somewhere
nearby, her mother is buried, and another, and another
woman's mother—someone my life depends on.

There is no book that can prove this,
just stories women tell you.

HOW I LEARNED TO COUNT

In the Ohio I know, the one nobody jokes about, Ralph Keefer
farms five hundred acres and holds on to that land
the way he grips a wrench. His right wrist,
cracked twenty years ago, has locked in place, so stiff
his arm and shoulder jerk and twist, half his body
devoted to the one small chore, tightening nut and bolt.

If there's a joke to tell here, it's on me, a college boy who
        once figured
he'd round up Keefer's heifer. One morning, sunny and dewy,
there she was like a statue in my yard, grazing on the tall grass.
Who could blame her? Not yet a year old, only half as high
as a man at her shoulder, white and black hide slipped tight
        around her
joints and slender neck, she simply longed after that unmown,
foot-high feast untrampled and so green it must have seemed
        heaven to a cow.

How she finagled her way through barbed wire
there's no telling, but that morning, I looked out my window
and knew what to do. I eased the door open to sneak
up and corral her. Forty feet between us, she swung her head
        toward me,
looked me over, the bristles on her chin moist, her jaw
grinding. Drooling at the corners of her mouth, she chewed
on what to make of me, no doubt, her wide eyes the size of walnuts.

I don't know how to talk to a cow. I know now there's no
pleading "Hey bossy, there, there, bossy," sidling closer, holding
out an empty hand. Even a tender-hoofed cow knows what
        you're up to.
And me? What I thought I'd do if I caught her I couldn't tell you.

Crook my arm around her neck? Haul her back to the fence,
    hold apart
the barbed wires while she sank to her knees, shimmied back
    to her pasture?

Lucky for me she kept her distance. So when I panicked,
figured I'd charge her, all there was to live down
was confessing to Keefer how I'd run off his heifer, last I saw
her back legs kicking up gravel and dirt a half-mile down our
    county road.

You go visit the Ohio I know. In Athens County, farmers swap
    this tale
about a cow that outsmarted a college man who couldn't figure
    simple arithmetic.
Ralph Keefer will tell you, if you dare hope hold on
to what you have, you must learn to count:
One man can tighten just one bolt at a time.
One acre yields two hundred bushel of corn or nothing.
One potent bull satisfies twelve heifers.
Most every time, four legs outrun two.

NEARING SIXTY, A MAN DECLARES HIMSELF A ROMANTIC

He wishes his wife would rise
from her patio chair, walk
next to him, sit on his lap. She might
whisper how the full moon
shines so beautifully, how
it is the color of his hair.

He wishes their son would visit
his garden. He would show him
this year's rows of green
beans, sweet corn, and
carrots—"Miracles,"
he would say.

He wishes their daughter would listen
to his stories and hear how
he tries to make his voice
slow and lonesome, like Benny
Goodman's sweet clarinet.

Does anyone know how he grieves
for the moon, or the way dirt
feels between his fingers? Does anyone
know the story he is writing
in his head, the hero
he would have been
when he was a boy?

Nearing sixty, he still loves
to fish the deep lakes near the house
where he was born. He wakes up
at dawn and does not return

until dark. Today, he climbs into
his small boat, dips oars
into the lake, and rows
the way his father taught him,
soundlessly, pulling
slowly against the weight of the water.

He wishes his father could see how his large
hands make perfect moons
in the air around him, how everything
circles back, how his whole body
rocks in heroic rhythm to his rowing.

NATURAL HISTORY

I squat where the grass grows
thick and soft, beside the pond
where trout swim near the horizon of air
and water, eyes like onyx pebbles,
mosquito or waterbug reflected there.

Ganglia tingle in the trout's brainstem—

what bolts down
spine, ribs, fins; the swift flip
of jawbone—

             which is the splash
that turns my head, that shocks me
before I know why, the glimpse
of tailfin, ripples in the water
where my father taught me to aim
my cast. This moment
I hunt
for whatever horizon there is
between history and my heart.

LOOKING FOR THE LANGUAGE OF WATER, WALKING, OF LOVE

Where I grew up in Ohio, my grandparents would have called this
     water I walk beside
a crick—a word my father also used for the ache in his back after
     he'd watered
and hoed his garden from sunrise to noon, his two boys dawdling
behind him, not worth a lick—also a word for where animals
     gather, so I've heard
about this place, Kelly Creek, where a twelve-point buck's craving
     might be settled.
I am in South Carolina, out State Route 56, where I think a man
     might beg
for a licking if he looked the wrong way at another man's wife
     or sister.
It was like that in Ohio, too.

In better English, you could say *stream*. You could say *spasm*. You could
describe piquant boys worthless to their father laboring in his garden.

You could say *brawl*.

I walk down Kelly Creek, keeping close to the water. I follow the
     path
I'm given, sometimes over slippery rocks, over sandbars, sometimes
     farther
from the bank, picking my way around trees, bamboo stalks, kudzu,
and briars—*prickers* I called them when I was a boy.
I love this walk today in South Carolina, a far piece from Ohio, or
     the walk last month
in the Blue Ridge Mountains with the woman I love, or in West
     Virginia
where I live now, where I dally as often as I can near the river
     and hills

at Valley Falls. This kind of walking, you keep your eyes to the
   ground—someone else
might think you were ashamed—but you just never know what will
   seize you, a kind of moss
you've never seen before, or gopher hole that would snap your
   ankle. You have to love
each step. You look for the rock that won't come loose, the root
   that will hold,
dirt that will pack down under your boot and won't slip where you
   dig in.
Nose to the ground, you pause. You stoop, squint down the seam of
   a raw pod
about to bust open, plump seeds so red you want to find a new
   name for that color,
not scarlet, *not* magenta, but something else, no word yet for what
   you've pinched between your fingers.

Should I have said *burst*?

There is a language people made for this place, for walking, and for
   love, an art
I'd like to hold onto, making words for what I find when I walk, for
   what keeps me
coming back to these creeks and gullies and hollers.

Spider's Lace. Knuckle stalks. Backbone stones.
Not gurgle, not babble, but how the water has a tongue that licks
inside my ear when I stand still, listen. *Feather moss.* The nervous bird
with no name, wings that waggle inside my chest
when I see the woman I love, like walking on water.

NO DOMINION

Across the East Coast of America, the honeybee—*Apis*
mellifera—has died. Mites have infested the hives:
the *varroa*, big enough to see, wedges in the creases
of a bee's body; the *tracheal mite*, microscopic
but more deadly, lodges in the throat, chokes.

Beekeepers' hives are empty. The fields
are quiet. No ecstatic buzz among dandelions
or black raspberries. In the white dutch clover
bees do not dance for each other, mapping the journey
to pollen and nectar. Keepers visit their silent
apiaries, nostalgic for living shelves of bees
they held between their gloved hands
like old priests at their altars.

On an island in the Chesapeake Bay, scientists breed
new queens from Yugoslavia, three hundred dollars
for one imported bee. They are packaged
and safe in tiny boxes, one bee each. Scientists experiment
with hybrids, resilient but gentle, their honey sweet.

Last week, a woman tells me, she found
among the deep-blue stars of borage
flowers, dancing among the leaves that taste
like cucumbers, honeybees, a small cloud
hovering and buzzing there. She does not know
where they come from—a wild hive, she guesses—bees
luckier, or stronger, than their engineered cousins,
a hive of *Apis mellifera* whose instinct and desire
are older than Roman words
for bee, honey, for what is born wild.

In my neighbor's yard, a pug dog sniffs
clipped grass. Its whole body swivels
in a circle, as if an axle plumbed
from the dog's center of gravity
straight through bedrock, magma,
down to the molten core.

And why not all the way to China?
Lingering in this breed is the scent
of the Emperor's hand massaging wrinkled skin
on the pug's neck, the Forbidden City's aromas—
silk, spice, incense, the familiar
odor of god idling on his gold throne.

Now the dog lies down, the whiff of mown grass
deep in its snout. The pug rolls and digs
its shoulder into the ground for the joy
of scratching that thick hide, its body
unfolding like West Virginia's hilly horizon.

AN EQUATION FOR HOFSTADTER

Now you may feel a little dizzy—but the best is yet to come.

—DOUGLAS HOFSTADTER,
*Gödel, Escher, Bach:
An Eternal Golden Braid*

On Backbone Mountain, the ridge
I drive across each day, I slow down
mornings winding
my way to work. The car
tilts into the curve's
ascent against mountainside.

Loggers' trucks grind gears. Pavement
blisters. At the berm, asphalt
crumbles and flakes, mixes
with gravel and cinder. The guardrail
is a cable as thick as my forefinger
strung between wooden posts
two feet high. You might be saved
if the cable twisted around
a wheel or bumper.

           The mountain road
is like the sand-track a desert snake makes:
a wave
of sine and cosine coiled
on a meridian. The fractal
path up the mountain
is like a dystrophied spine.

Slow down. I promise
the mountain gives ground enough.

NOTES

"In the Church of Saint Stephen": See Acts 7:51: "As your fathers did, so do you."

"Stories a Man Keeps to Himself": The word *wasichu* is used as a racial slur, a usage glossed over in *Black Elk Speaks*. John G. Neihardt provides only this note: "A term used to designate the white man, but having no reference to the color of his skin." I use the word to mean "other" or "stranger," but I must also accept the slur: "I have no right / to that man's life . . . I am Wasichu . . . ."

"The Men of Springtime": When I take essential terms or phrases from Barry Lopez's *Arctic Dreams*, I try to acknowledge with italics or quotation marks where these do not interfere with the poem. I am indebted to Lopez for his marvelous book.

"A Japanese Woman Confides in Me and Speaks of Heaven" is for Masumi, a former student of mine at Fairmont State College in West Virginia, who wrote the lovely essay from which this poem steals much of its language and all of the story.

The sequence "Three Short Clay Poems" is for Jack Troy, who once admonished me to write a short poem for a change. "A Clay Bowl" was the result, to which Jack responded, "I like it but I think it needs to be longer." Hence, *three* short clay poems.

Three Poems for One Traveler is for my wife, Libby Davis.

Cafe Negro at Soda Pininini is dedicated to Lloyd Wright Daley and his wife, Rosa, who owned the *Soda* (lunch counter) near Cahuita, Costa Rica, where one could find a good cup of black coffee, hear (in English and Spanish) Lloyd's lively stories and Rosa's good advice, use the public phone to call family and friends anywhere in the world, and flag down the bus to San José. Thanks also to Winston McCloud, who knows about a lot more than lizards.

"Naming Day" and "Where the Children Go" are *in memoriam,* Wilhelm ("Bill") Lichtenwald, my mother's father. The Lichtenwald family is descended from the Volga Germans who retained their native culture and language after they emigrated to Russia's Volga River Valley.

"How I Learned to Count" is for Ralph Keefer, a storyteller and leg puller.

"No Dominion": Thanks to Valerie Nieman and John King, bee charmers both.

Saguaro ecology affected by cutting ironwood, Ejido San Ignacio. Photograph by David Burckhalter.

OCCASIONAL PAPERS IN CONSERVATION BIOLOGY

Ironwood:
An Ecological and Cultural Keystone
of the Sonoran Desert

Edited by
Gary Paul Nabhan
John L. Carr

CONSERVATION INTERNATIONAL
OCCASIONAL PAPER NO. 1
APRIL 1994

Published by Conservation International

*Conservation International is a private,
nonprofit organization exempt from
federal income tax under
section 501(c)(3) of the
Internal Revenue Code*

CONSERVATION INTERNATIONAL
Department of Conservation Biology
1015 18th Street, NW Suite 1000
Washington, DC 20036 USA
Tel: 202/429-5660
Fax: 202/887-0193

Managing Editor: **John L. Carr**
Design: **Kim Awbrey**
Cover Art: **Delphine Keim**
Paul Mirocha

Library of Congress Catalog No. 94-70016
ISBN 1-881173-07-0

*Printed on Recycled Paper in
theUnited States of America*

Table of Contents

Dedicated to

Dr. Alwyn H. Gentry (1945 - 1993)

and

Dr. Howard Scott Gentry (1904 - 1993)

explorers of Latin American floras
and their cultural uses

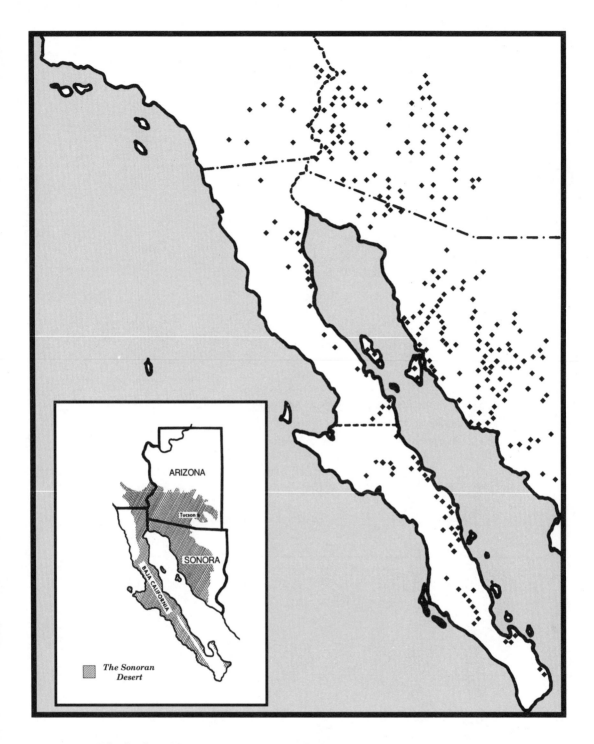

Distribution of ironwood (*Olneya tesota*) with an inset of the Sonoran Desert.

INTRODUCTION

Gary Paul Nabhan and Mark J. Plotkin

This collection of four studies from the Sonoran Desert deals with ancient desert legumes (some of them up to 1200 years old) and their effects on both biological and cultural diversity.

The Sonoran Desert is the least barren of arid lands in the Americas, and is characterized by the greatest diversity of growth forms of any desert in the world. It is well-known internationally for its giant cacti, but these monstrous succulents are in turn dependent upon ancient legume trees which serve as "nurse plants" to create favorable microhabitats for their dispersal, germination, seedling establishment and survival. Our preliminary surveys indicate that more than 160 plant species, including six threatened succulents, depend upon legumes such as ironwood (*Olneya*) and mesquite (*Prosopis*) for their regeneration in the Sonoran Desert. Endangered wildlife species such as the Sonoran pronghorn antelope, desert bighorn and masked bobwhite quail also depend upon these two legumes for shelter and forage.

Here we focus on *Olneya,* a monotypic genus. It serves as a habitat-modifying keystone critical to the structure and function of the Sonoran Desert. Although not endangered as a species—its range covers several million hectares and it is represented by hundreds of thousands of individuals—its rapid depletion and low rates of regeneration have become concerns of many desert ecologists. In 1991, Conservation International's Plant Conservation Program sponsored the formation of the Ironwood Alliance, a binational task force of scientists, businessmen, artists, journalists and activists who wished to assess the ecological and cultural impacts of ironwood (and mesquite) depletion, and to propose alternatives to continued destruction. To date, the Alliance has not only sponsored the fine research included in this monograph, but has led public awareness and political action campaigns to reduce the threats to ancient legume habitats in Sonora, Arizona, and Baja California Sur. SEDESOL has recently decreed ironwood a protected species in the Republic of México and is providing additional enforcement and monitoring of this natural resource. Another agency, SECOFI, is working with us to provide assistance to Seri Indian carvers who have been impacted by the increasing scarcity of ironwood on the Sonoran coast of the Sea of Cortez.

All of the Alliance's applied conservation efforts have been based upon the scientific understanding of ironwood's importance to biological and cultural diversity, yet this monograph is our first opportunity to present our findings in a comprehensive and detailed form. As readers will quickly notice, many of the issues dealt with by Ironwood Alliance researchers are vital global issues in the field of conservation biology: the definition of keystone species; the effects of habitat fragmentation; the measure of biodiversity; the estimation of recovery times for damaged ecosystems; and the human impacts on the demography of rare species. In particular, we have attempted to address conservation problems in and near biosphere reserves, and those which affect indigenous peoples, who are threatened cultural and "genetic" entities themselves.

It is clear from the conclusions made by contributing authors that solutions for these problems must come not only from biology, but also from resource economics, cultural anthropology, ethics and conservation activism. We have presented our findings to the Arizona-México Commission, the Mexican government, professional scientific societies, local communities and the media. SEDESOL's recent decree of ironwood as a protected keystone will hopefully provide additional enforcement and monitoring of this vulnerable natural resource. Yet it will take continuing international cooperation to reduce the threats to ironwood habitats and their attendant organisms, for the pressures on these habitats are being generated from both sides of the U.S./ México boundary.

We thank the Pew Scholars Program in Conservation and Environment, the Overbrook Foundation, the Robidaux Foundation, the ARCO Foundation, John Hay, Jim Hills, Roy Young, and other anonymous donors for their contributions to this field research and its publication. We are also grateful for the assistance provided by Conservation International's Washington, D.C. staff in seeing this publication reach fruition, especially Kim Awbrey, Robin Bell, Lisa Famolare, Gina Fognani, Adrian Forsyth, Enrique Ortiz, Regina de Souza, and Melida Tajbakhsh.

INTRODUCCIÓN

Esta publicación comprende la colección de cuatro estudios sobre las leguminosas arborescentes más antiguas en el Desierto Sonorense. Estos árboles llegan a sobrevivir hasta 1200 años y tienen efectos cruciales en la diversidad biológica y cultural.

El Desierto Sonorense constituye el más tropical de los desiertos de Norteamérica. Se caracteriza por ser un territorio que presenta la mayor biodiversidad en regiones áridas en términos de forma de vida y endemismo. Es famoso por su internacionalmente conocidos "cactus columnares." Para sobrevivir, éstos gigantes suculentes dependen de plantas nodrizas o "madrinas." La mayoría consiste de árboles leguminosos que proporcionan protección y nutrición a plantas aledañas creando un ambiente favorable para la germinación y sobrevivencia de plantulas. Nuestros estudios preliminares indican que más de 160 especies de plantas, incluyendo seis consideradas como amenazadas, dependen del palo fierro (*Olneya tesota*) y del mezquite (*Prosopis*) para su regeneración en el Desierto Sonorense. Especies endémicas como el berrendo Sonorense, el borrego cimarrón, y la codorníz mascarita, también dependen de la sombra crucial así como de las ramas y follaje que proporcionan éstas plantas leguminosas.

En particular, nos concentramos en el papel que el palo fierro (*Olneya tesota*) juega como modificador clave (keystone) para la estructura y función del ecosistema que comprende el Desierto Sonorense. *Olneya* es un género monotípico del Desierto Sonorense. Los ecólogos no consideran ésta especie en peligro de extinción, debido a que su extensión abarca milliones de hectáreas y sus poblaciones contienen miles de individuos. Sin embargo, su rápido desmonte, sobreexplotación y baja regeneración son causas de alarmas.

En 1991, el programa de Plantas de Conservación Internacional y el programa México financiaron la creación de la Alianza Pro Palo Fierro, que consiste en un comité bi-nacional con la participación de científicos, comerciantes, artistas indígenas, periodistas y activistas. La Alianza Pro Palo Fierro ha promulgado y promulga la necesidad de evaluar el impacto crítico, tanto ecológico, como cultural y económico de la sobreexplotación del palo fierro y mezquite, a la vez que proponer alternativas a ésta continua destrucción. Actualmente, la Alianza no solamente ha financiado estudios de investigación, si no que ha establecido una campaña de comunicación a través de medios de difusión local, creando conciencia pública y logrando que se planifiquen campañas de acción política. El propósito de éstas es el de reducir las amenazas contra la pérdida de los valores ecológicos de las leguminosas antiguas en Sonora, Arizona, y Baja California Sur. Recientemente, la agencia del gobierno Mexicano SEDESOL ha decretado palo fierro como una especie protegida en la República, y está proporcionando vigilancia adicional sobre éste vulnerable recurso natural. Otra agencia participante es SECOFI, con la cual trabajamos en conjunto para promover asistencia a los indígenas de la tribu Seri. Los Seris son artesanos talladores que habitan en las costas del Mar de Cortez en Sonora. Los Seri han sufrido grandes pérdidas económicas por la disminución del palo fierro el cual utilizan como material para tallar las artesanías de cuya venta obtienen rendimientos económicos.

Los esfuerzos de la Alianza para la conservación del palo fierro han sido basados en el reconocimiento de los valores biológicos de ésta especie y su papel en la diversidad cultural. Esta monografía nos brinda la primera oportunidad de presentar nuestros hallazgos en una forma más detallada. Los lectores podrán ratificar que los temas escogidos por los investigadores de la Alianza Pro Palo Fierro son temas de óptima importancia global en campos como: la conservación biológica, la definición de especies claves, los efectos de la fragmentación del hábitat, las inestabilidades causadas por la interrupción del mutualismo, la medida de la biodiversidad, la estimación de la recuperación de ecosistemas dañados y el impacto humano sobre la demografía de especies raras. En particular, nos hemos propuesto identificar los problemas de conservación en las áreas protegidas y las reservas de biosfera cercanas que afectan tanto genéticamente a las plantas que se encuentran en éstas áreas, como a los grupos étnicos que en ellas habitan.

En base a las conclusiones presentadas por los autores contribuyentes, se comprueba claramente que la solución a éstos problemas no puede venir solamente de la ciencia biológica, si no que también deben considerarse los recursos económicos, culturales, antropológicos, así como aspectos éticos de la conservación. Hemos presentado los resultados de nuestras investigaciones ante la Comisión Arizona-Sonora, del gobierno Mexicano, sociedades científicas profesionales, comunidades locales y ante los medios de difusión. El decreto reciente de SECOFI, cuyo propósito es proteger el palo fierro como clave del ecosistema desértico de la República Mexicana, proveerá más vigilancia y monitoreo sobre éste recurso susceptible. Sin embargo, necesitamos continua cooperación para proteger el palo fierro y mezquite, claves en el ecosistema y especies que sustentan varias formas de vida animal y vegetal, así como para aliviar las presiones generadas en ambos lados de la frontera y los alrededores de éstos hábitats.

Agradecemos al programa "Pew Scholars in Conservation and Environment," a "Overbrook Foundation," a "Robidaux Foundation," a "Arco Foundation," John Hay, Jim Hills, Roy Young y a otros donantes anónimos que han contribuido a éstos estudios, investigación y publicación. Estamos especialmente agradecidos con el personal de Conservación Internacional, Washington, DC, por su apoyo y cooperación en hacer ésta publicación un realidad, en particular: Kim Awbrey, Robin Bell, Lisa Famolare, Gina Fognani, Adrian Forsyth, Enrique Ortiz, Regina de Souza y Melida Tajbakhsh.

ISLANDS OF DIVERSITY: IRONWOOD ECOLOGY AND THE RICHNESS OF PERENNIALS IN A SONORAN DESERT BIOLOGICAL RESERVE

Alberto Búrquez and María de los Angeles Quintana

ABSTRACT

This study explores the influence of ironwood trees (*Olneya tesota*) on the diversity of perennials in the continental southern half of the Sonoran Desert. It was found that ironwood density varies considerably between sites; from 29 to 109 trees ha^{-1}. Older classes of ironwood do bear marks of past woodcutting episodes. Most of the human impact in this population was traceable to heavy pruning at the turn of the century. Younger trees (ca. 70 yr or less) do not show evidence of damage by woodcutters. Despite the heavy historic use, the trees have regained their typical canopy morphology after a few decades of recovery time. From the structure of size classes, recruitment seems to occur in episodes well separated in time.

The richness of perennial species under the shade of ironwood trees is about twice that of equivalent areas beyond their shade. Of 65 species of perennials identified in the sampling, 52 occur in the shade of ironwood, 31 are found associated only with ironwood, and 25 seem to be independent of it. Additionally, eight species were never found in its shade. The shade of ironwood not only promotes a higher species richness, but a greater diversity or heterogeneity of underlings. Most of the variation in species diversity can be explained by the effects of ironwood acting as a "nurse plant" for many perennials. However, a small, but highly significant variation in diversity can also be ascribed to the features of the environment (site effects). The environmental modifications caused by a "nurse plant" are diverse, but plants under the ironwood's shade are generally better protected from damaging radiation and predation, and grow in more humid and fertile soil. Its presence as a refugium for birds and mammals can, in turn, aid in the dispersal of propagules adapted to their handling. The most pervasive threat to the stability of this community is the introduction of exotic buffel grass (*Cenchrus ciliaris*), which rapidly accumulates combustible litter. When burning occurs, ironwood trees burn down entirely and the arborescent desert is replaced by a dry grassland where virtually no recruitment of perennials has been recorded to date.

RESÚMEN

Este estudio explora el papel de los árboles de palo fierro (*Olneya tesota*) en la diversidad de perennes en la porción sur continental del Desierto Sonorense. Se encontró que la densidad de palo fierro varía ampliamente, desde 29 hasta 109 árboles ha⁻¹. Poco menos de la mitad de los árboles presenta marcas de corte para su uso como leña. El uso puede trazarse historicamente a principios de siglo. Los árboles jóvenes (ca. 70 años o menos) no muestran evidencias de daño. A pesar de este severo uso de la población, los árboles recuperan su morfología después de unas cuantas décadas. Del estudio de la estructura de tamaños, el reclutamiento parece darse en episodios bien separados en el tiempo.

La riqueza de perennes bajo su copa es de aproximadamente el doble de áreas fuera de la copa. De 65 especies identificadas, 52 ocurren bajo su copa, 31 se encuentran directamente asociadas al palo fierro, 25 parecen tener una distribución independiente y ocho nunca se encontraron asociadas. La sombra del palo fierro promueve, no sólo una mayor riqueza de especies, sino una mayor diversidad. Gran parte de la variación en diversidad puede explicarse por el "nodriza" que juega el palo fierro en el reclutamiento y permanencia de muchas perennes. Sin embargo, una porción pequeña pero altamente significativa en la diversidad, puede explicarse por los efectos de sitio. Las causas del efecto "nodriza" tienen un orígen múltiple, pero en general, las plantas bajo su copa están mejor protegidas de la insolación y depredación, y crecen en ambientes más fértiles y húmedos. Su presencia como refugio de aves y pequeños mamíferos puede ser importante para algunas especies dispersadas por estos animales. La principal amenaza a la estabilidad de la comunidad es probablemente la introducción del zacate Sudafricano "buffel" (*Cenchrus ciliaris*), el cual rápidamente acumula hojarasca combustible. Cuando ocurre un fuego, los árboles de palo fierro se queman totalmente y la comunidad arborescente es reemplazada por un pastizal seco en el que casi no ocurre reclutamiento de perennes.

INTRODUCTION

The distribution of organisms in nature is usually aggregated. The environment is a patchwork of varying physical and biological factors. At the physical level, topography, rockiness, nutrient levels, water availability, air and soil temperature and other factors vary as patches (Kareiva 1986). This phenomenon is apparent at different spatial and temporal scales (Wiens et al. 1986). Disturbances also modify environments in a patchy manner, and even the presence of a single, large organism, such as a tree, can modify the physical and biological environment by changing the microclimate and promoting a network of biological interactions beneath the canopy. These interactions are largely concentrated within the area of cover, but extend into the rhizosphere and often influence competition for several meters beyond the canopy shadow of the tree.

Metaphorically, the discrete canopies of trees in the desert are islands or gaps in forests. Canopies and gaps offer special habitats for a variety of species that do not occur in other locations. Gap dynamics in forests are well studied in temperate and tropical communities (see Brokaw 1982; Hubbell and Foster 1985, 1986; Dirzo et al. 1992). This heuristic device or metaphor can be "inverted" or extended to the study of open communities, in which the "gaps" could be considered as the areas covered by the crowns of dispersed trees.

Most forms of population interaction can be found when examining the effects of shade under long-lived trees. One common consequence of life beneath a tree canopy is a decrease in growth or recruitment of underlying species. This may be due to the blocking of light, as found in tropical forests (Brokaw 1982, Alvarez-Buylla and Martínez-Ramos 1992); or due to the combination of allelopathic and competitive effects

(Bartholomew 1970). In biotic communities like deserts in which competition for light or nutrients does not seem to form the main structuring axis of the community (see Tilman 1986), other positive interactions can be found (Wilson 1986). One such axis is the escape from damaging radiation and from high temperature at the soil surface of the desert, resulting in a better availability of soil moisture under the crown of trees (Halvorson and Patten 1975, Patten 1978). A classic case of this interaction is the nurse plant effect in the recruitment of saguaro (*Carnegiea gigantea*) and other columnar cacti (Turner et al. 1966, Steenbergh and Lowe 1977, Valiente-Banuet and Ezcurra 1991).

From the point of view of annuals and short-lived perennials, the presence of ironwood or other nurses can be compared to other shade-bearing features of the physical environment. In this paper, we study the population structure of ironwood trees and the effect of their permanence on the diversity of perennials under their canopy. We hypothesize that the permanence of ironwood trees has promoted an increase in the diversity of species under their crowns. Our aim is to discern the role of ironwood trees as "islands" of diversity. Here, we present data on how the diversity of perennials is affected by the shade of ironwood trees. In forthcoming papers, spring and summer annuals will be addressed, and the role of artificial grasslands on diminishing biodiversity will be evaluated.

MATERIALS AND METHODS

1. Autecology

Following mesquite (*Prosopis*) and cottonwood (*Populus*) that dominate riparian corridors along rivers and large streams, the ironwood (*Olneya tesota* Gray) is the largest tree in the Sonoran Desert, reaching up to 14 m in height. It grows in the most xeric parts of the desert and is seldom confined to drainage channels as happens with other arborescent species of the desert. Nevertheless, it reaches its largest dimensions along the small arroyos or ephemeral watercourses in the desert (Felger

and Moser 1985). In terms of its contribution to above-ground biomass, ironwood is among the five most important species of the region by virtue of its large size and the high specific gravity of its wood (1.22; Búrquez et al. 1992).

Mature trees may be either single or multi-trunked. Near the base, ironwoods produce suckers from the roots and straight, vigorous young branches. In the southern Sonoran Desert, ironwood trees are never leafless, but a perceptible leaf fall has been observed during most of the year (A. Martínez-Yrízar, pers. comm). Large pools of organic matter in various stages of decomposition are conspicuous under their canopies, where the soil profiles sharply contrast with those of barren mineral soils of the open desert. Ironwood flowers are pale lavender, purple, or pinkish. Flowering begins in March, and usually is followed by a brief mast of pods mature by early summer. Pod production is episodic, peaking every few years. The large seeds are contained in a short pod, and vary from one to four seeds per pod. These are eaten by a variety of mammals. Some are gathered and reserved in caches by small mammals; if not eaten immediately, they may germinate after the rains in aggregates. Most of the seedlings die after germinating because of the lack of continuous moisture, suggesting that recruitment may take place as rare episodic events every few decades. In a survey of more than 4 ha in our study area, no established seedlings were found in two consecutive years of diligent searching. In the greenhouse, plants readily grow, reaching a height of more than 1 m in less than three years.

2. Study Sites

The study sites are located in the biological reserve of the Centro Ecológico de Sonora, 2.5 km south of the city of Hermosillo, Sonora, México. The vegetation of this small reserve (less than 600 ha) belongs to the Plains of Sonora subdivision of the Sonoran Desert (Shreve and Wiggins 1964, Hastings et al. 1972). The area was characterized by Shreve (1951) as the most typical habitat of ironwood, which he termed as the *Encelia-Olneya* association. Geomorphologically, the sites are located on arid plains intersected by many small drainage channels and hills formed by massive granitic outcrops. The sandy soils have montmorillonite clays derived from the decomposition of the granite. These are classed mainly as Lithosols, Yermosols, and Xerosols.

Ironwood occurs in three of the five major types of vegetation in the area (Búrquez, Martínez, Quijada and Castillo, in prep.). Typical vegetation associations that include ironwood are: 1) the Plains of Sonora subdivision of the Sonoran Desert, with *Encelia* and *Olneya* as the dominants, and 2) Plains of Sonora Xeroriparian. This latter association is more diverse than the former, occurring only along small ephemeral watercourses. It is devoid of strongly dominant species, and contains many arborescent co-dominants, including: *Olneya tesota*, *Bursera* spp., *Guaiacum coulteri*, and *Eysenhardtia orthocarpa*, and shrubs like *Jatropha cordifolia*, *Mimosa laxiflora*, *Caesalpinia palmeri* and *Randia obcordata*. This association is also rich in vines including: three spp. of *Janusia*, *Mascagnia macroptera*, *Cardiospermum corindum*, *Marsdenia edulis*, *Matelea cordifolia*, *Sarcostemma cynanchoides*, *Merremia palmeri*, *Ipomoea leptotoma*, *Phaseolus filiformis*, *Nissolia schottii*, and *Aristolochia watsonii* among others. Ironwood does not occur either on slopes of greater than 20%, which are mainly the domain of tropical thornscrub, or along the large watercourses where mesquite gallery forests have been established.

3. Population Structure

To cover a range of conditions, four sites of 1 ha each were arbitrarily selected. Two of them were located in the plains — flat terrains subjected only to sheet flooding (sites 2 and 3) — and two in the lowermost parts exposed to occasional runoff from temporary small arroyos (sites 1 and 4). In each site all individuals of ironwood were mapped, and the following attributes were recorded: 1) diameter of the canopy along two perpendicular axes, the first one aligned N-S; 2) number of trunks at ground surface; 3) diameter of each trunk at ground surface; 4)

maximum height; and 5) evidence of damage from slashing from past woodcutting or pruning. Cover was estimated by fitting an ellipse to the two canopy diameters. Total basal area at ground level was estimated by summing the individual basal areas for all trunks.

4. Community Structure of Perennials

From all ironwood individuals at each site, a random sample of three canopy cover classes was drawn: small (1-15 m^2), intermediate (20-35 m^2), and large (40 m^2 or more). For each of the small and intermediate classes, five individuals were randomly selected, and six were selected for the large class. The same procedure was followed to select identical areas outside ironwood canopies in each site. Each sampling area (outside or under ironwood trees) represented a "plot," in which the abundance of perennial species was recorded using a modified relevè method (Mueller-Dumbois and Ellenberg 1974). The cover of each species was given the following scale values: 5 = more than 3/4 of the canopy cover; 4 = 1/2-3/4; 3 = 1/4-1/2; 2 = 1/20-1/4; and 5 = negligible-1/20 (Braun-Blanquet 1965). These values were later transformed to relative abundance by dividing them by the cumulative sum of values in each plot. Given the relative abundances per plot, histograms of species occurrence and abundance were produced for each size class at each site. The maximum number of species and the mean values of relative abundance were presented for each size class. Diversity, measured as the heterogeneity of the abundance of the various species present (Peet 1974) was calculated using the Shannon-Wiener information index (Mueller-Dumbois and Ellenberg 1974). An analysis of variance (ANOVA) was performed using the cover area of each plot as a covariate in a regression model. This allowed us to test for differences in the curves of diversity-area for each site beneath and outside the canopies of ironwood.

These data offer snapshots of ironwood associations at different points in space and time, and therefore serve as "natural experiments" in the sense of Diamond (1986). The ability to match sites was maximized by selecting four sites and comparing plots of the same size under and outside of ironwood canopies. Independent variables were clearly differentiated, allowing for great control. As a "snapshot" experiment, it allows the comparison of the effects of shade and site, while the effect of the size of trees works as a trajectory along which one can measure the effects of time.

RESULTS

1. Population Structure

Ironwood populations in the study area vary in density from sites where no ironwood trees are present to those where the densities are very high. In our samples, density varied from 29 to 109 individuals ha^{-1} (Site 1=34, 2=29, 3=35, 4=109). Oral history from elderly residents living nearby the area indicate that the ironwood populations close to Hermosillo were heavily exploited for wood around the turn of the century (1890-1920). The wood was mainly used as part of a subsistence economy, but large ironwood stands nearby were cut to fuel the steam engines running from Hermosillo to the mining town of La Colorada, 50 km to the southeast. In our four sample sites, about half of the trees bear old ax marks almost at ground level, either on the main trunk or on large old branches (site 1=47%, site 2=55%, site 3=60%, site 4=62%). There is no evidence of recent cutting, and most of these marks of pruning are probably more than 70 years old.

The number of trunks per tree varies from 1 to 20, but trees with 1-2 trunks were the most common (Fig. 1). The number of trunks per tree is noticeably smaller in

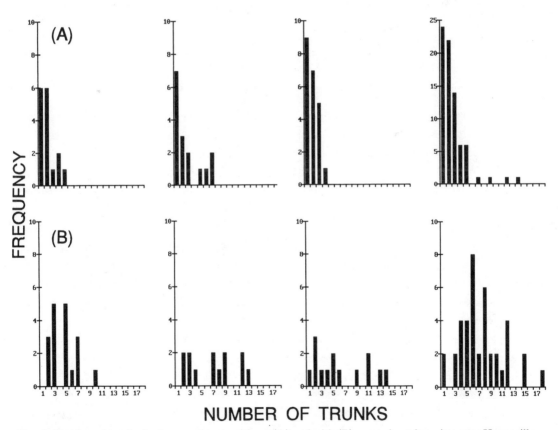

FIG. 1. Number of trunks for ironwood trees without (A) and with (B) ax marks at four sites near Hermosillo, Sonora, México. Sites in columns 1 and 3 on dry level terrain, sites in columns 2 and 4 along small temporary desert arroyos.

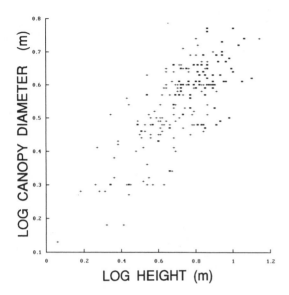

FIG. 2. Allometric relationship between the mean diameter of the crown and maximum height of ironwood trees with and without ax marks at four sites near Hermosillo, Sonora, México. Solid squares = without marks; crosses = with marks. The shape of the curves is not statistically different between sites or between trees cut or uncut, see text.

trees without ax marks than those with marks (Fig. 1). These findings support the hypothesis that multi-trunk trees are produced by human disturbance, rather than being naturally produced by dieback. Mature, undisturbed populations of ironwood in this area should be dominated by single, or few-trunked trees.

In allometric terms, ironwood trees grow rapidly upward and only later develop horizontally to form a crown. Young trees are narrow and tall, while old trees show a broader morphology. This phenomenon is demonstrated by plotting the allometric relation between the logarithms of the mean diameter of the crown and height (Fig. 2). Trees that show evidence of past cutting are larger, probably reflecting the fact that they sprouted from an established rootstock, while trees without marks are on the average smaller, suggesting that they were too young to be worth cutting when these populations were harvested. No significant differences were found when comparing the slopes of the curves of cut and uncut trees

$(t=1.94; p>0.05)$, and no discernible differences between sites were apparent. Old trees, when pruned, regain their morphology within a few decades. Then, irrespective of whether they have been cut or not, the trees follow a growth curve of the form $y=bx^k$:

$$\text{Mean diameter} = 0.2167 + \text{height}^{0.460}$$

The cover of the canopies follows a highly skewed distribution, with the smallest classes better represented, and wide gaps occurring between the largest classes (Fig. 3). This distribution approaches a more normal distribution when transformed to a logarithmic scale. However, there is an excess of intermediate values, suggesting a leptokurtic log-normal distribution of cover areas, with some peaks extending beyond the idealized curve. The distribution of total basal area follows a curve similar to that of cover (Fig. 3). Conversely, height on an arithmetic scale approaches a more normally distributed curve (Fig. 3).

2. Community Structure

I. Species richness

A total of 65 species of perennials was found inside and outside the shade of ironwood trees. Of these, 31 (48%) seem to be closely associated with the microenvironment provided by ironwoods (Table 1). *Commelina erecta, Physalis crassifolia, Lantana horrida, Lophocereus schottii, Stenocereus thurberi, Abutilon* sp., *Guaiacum coulteri* and *Celtis pallida* occured only in the deep shade of the largest trees. Several climbers were mostly found under ironwoods, including *Ibervillea sonorae, Aristolochia watsonii, Nissolia schottii, Matelea cordifolia,* and *Lantana horrida.* Other scandent species occur with a much higher frequency under ironwoods than outside its shade: *Peniocereus striatus, Stegnosperma halmifolium, Commicarpus scandens, Phaulothamnus spinescens, Colubrina viridis* and the three species of *Lycium* in the area. In addition to the *Peniocereus* discussed by Suzán et al. (in press), several species of Cactaceae show a definite preference for ironwood trees, including *Lophocereus schottii* and *Stenocereus thurberi,*

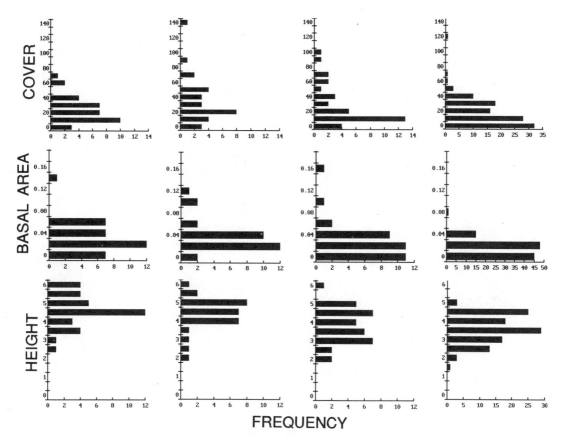

FIG. 3. Frequency distribution of canopy area cover (top row), basal area (middle row), and maximum height (lower row) of ironwood trees at four sites near Hermosillo, Sonora, México. Sites in columns 1 and 3 on dry level terrain, sites in columns 2 and 4 along small temporary desert arroyos. Cover and basal area in m², maximum height in m.

and the small *Mammillaria mainae* and *M. grahamii*. Saplings and immature ironwood trees were found only under the shade of their large forebears.

A few species of perennials (13%) were never found under ironwood trees, growing preferentially in exposed situations along the banks of arroyos (*Bursera fagaroides, Stenocereus alamosensis, Acacia occidentalis* and *Desmanthus covillei*), on gentle slopes (*Jatropha cordata, Marina parryi* and *Cercidium microphyllum*), or where there is complete exposure (*Cathestecum erectum*).

Twenty-five species (39%) of plants failed to show association with ironwoods. *Encelia farinosa, Croton sonorae, Mimosa laxiflora*, and *Jatropha cardiophylla*

are the most noticeable taxa in terms of abundance. Important shrubby and arborescent species are *Bursera laxiflora, Caesalpinia palmeri, Coursetia glandulosa, Eysenhardtia orthocarpa, Fouquieria macdougalii, Justicia californica, Karwinskia parvifolia, Krameria parviflora*, and *Randia obcordata*. Several climbers show no preference for ironwood, these include *Janusia californica, J. linearis, Cardiospermum corindum* and *Mascagnia macroptera*. The exotic buffel grass (*Cenchrus ciliaris*) has invaded every microenvironment as a result of its repeated and widespread introduction beginning almost 35 years ago.

Three species of *Bursera* occur sympatrically. On our sites, *B. microphylla* occurs only under ironwood

TABLE 1. Species found in plots of small (1), medium (2) and large (3) size, under (IN) or outside (OUT) the shade of ironwood trees in the southern Sonoran Desert (see methods). No. = reference number for each species in Fig. 4, 0 = absent, 1 = present. Data pooled from four neighboring sites; two influenced by a small arroyo and two on level terrain. n = 20 for each plot size, except plot size 3, with n = 24.

No. Species	IN	OUT	No. Species	IN	OUT
PLOT SIZE	3 2 1	3 2 1	PLOT SIZE	3 2 1	3 2 1
1 *Abutilon incanum*	1 1 0	1 1 1	34 *Jatropha cardiophylla*	1 1 1	1 1 1
2 *Abutilon* sp.	1 1 0	0 0 0	35 *Jatropha cordata*	0 0 0	1 1 0
3 *Acacia occidentalis*	0 0 0	1 0 0	36 *Justicia californica*	1 1 1	1 1 1
4 *Ambrosia ambrosioides*	1 0 1	0 0 0	37 *Karwinskia parvifolia*	1 1 1	1 1 0
5 *Apodanthera* sp.	1 0 0	0 0 0	38 *Krameria parviflora*	1 0 1	1 1 0
6 *Aristida ternipes*	1 0 0	0 0 0	39 *Lantana horrida*	1 0 0	0 0 0
7 *Aristolochia watsonii*	1 1 1	0 0 0	40 *Lophocereus schottii*	1 1 1	0 0 0
8 *Brickellia coulteri*	1 0 0	1 1 0	41 *Lycium andersonii*	1 1 0	0 0 0
9 *Bursera fagaroides*	0 0 0	1 0 0	42 *Lycium berlandieri*	1 0 0	1 0 0
10 *Bursera laxiflora*	1 1 1	1 1 1	43 *Lycium* sp.	1 0 0	0 0 0
11 *Bursera microphylla*	1 1 1	0 0 0	44 *Mammillaria grahamii*	0 1 0	0 0 0
12 *Caesalpinia palmeri*	1 0 1	1 1 1	45 *Mammillaria mainae*	1 0 0	0 0 0
13 *Cardiospermum corindum*	1 1 1	1 1 1	46 *Marina parryi*	0 0 1	0 0 0
14 *Cathestecum erectum*	0 0 0	1 0 0	47 *Mascagnia macroptera*	1 1 0	1 1 0
15 *Celtis pallida*	1 0 0	0 0 0	48 *Matelea cordifolia*	1 1 1	1 0 0
16 *Cenchrus ciliaris*	1 1 1	1 1 1	49 *Merremia palmeri*	1 1 1	1 0 0
17 *Cercidium microphyllum*	0 0 0	0 1 0	50 *Mimosa laxiflora*	1 1 1	1 1 1
18 *Colubrina viridis*	1 1 0	0 0 0	51 *Nissolia schottii*	1 0 1	0 0 0
19 *Commelina erecta*	1 0 0	0 0 0	52 *Olneya tesota*	1 1 0	0 0 0
20 *Commicarpus scandens*	1 1 0	0 0 0	53 *Opuntia arbuscula*	1 1 1	1 1 1
21 *Coursetia glandulosa*	1 0 1	1 1 0	54 *Opuntia fulgida mammillata*	1 1 1	1 1 1
22 *Croton sonorae*	1 1 1	1 1 1	55 *Opuntia leptocaulis*	1 1 1	1 1 0
23 *Cuscuta* sp.	0 1 0	0 0 0	56 *Peniocereus striatus*	0 1 0	0 0 0
25 *Desmanthus covilleii*	0 0 0	1 0 0	57 *Phaulothamnus spinescens*	1 1 1	0 0 0
26 *Encelia farinosa*	1 1 1	1 1 1	58 *Phoradendron californicum*	1 1 1	0 0 0
27 *Euphorbia polycarpa*	0 1 0	1 0 0	59 *Physalis* sp.	1 0 0	0 0 0
28 *Eysenhardtia orthocarpa*	1 1 0	1 0 1	60 *Randia obcordata*	1 1 1	1 1 0
29 *Fouquieria macdougalli*	1 1 0	1 0 0	61 *Setaria macrostachya*	1 0 0	0 0 0
30 *Guaiacum coulteri*	1 1 1	1 0 0	62 *Stegnosperma halmifolium*	1 1 0	0 0 0
31 *Ibervillea sonorae*	1 1 1	0 0 0	63 *Stenocereus alamosensis*	0 0 0	1 0 0
32 *Janusia californica*	1 1 1	1 1 1	64 *Stenocereus thurberi*	1 0 0	0 0 0
33 *Janusia linearis*	1 1 1	1 0 1	65 *Trixis californica*	1 1 1	0 1 0
			TOTAL SPECIES	52 39 31	34 23 15

TABLE 2. Similarity matrix comprising all the species found at four sites where ironwood occurs. The main diagonal indicates the number of species in each plot size (see Table 1), either under or outside canopies of ironwood. Values below the main diagonal are the common species, while above it the similarity ratio using the Sorensen index. n = 20 for each plot size, except plot size 3, with n = 24.

		UNDER			OUTSIDE		
		3	**2**	**1**	**3**	**2**	**1**
	3	52	.77	.72	.63	.56	.42
UNDER	**2**	35	39	.71	.63	.55	.52
	1	30	25	31	.62	.67	.57
	3	27	23	20	34	.74	.61
OUTSIDE	**2**	21	17	18	21	23	.68
	1	14	14	13	15	13	15

trees, *B. fagaroides* only outside, and *B. laxiflora* seems to be distributed independently of ironwood trees.

II. Similarity between plots

A similarity matrix using the Sorensen index shows that the greatest similarities in floristic composition exist between plots located under ironwood (upper-left quarter on Table 2), or between plots outside ironwoods (lower-right quarter), while the least similarity is found when comparing plots under ironwood with those outside their canopies (upper-right and lower-left quarters in Table 2). About 70% similarity occurs for plots inside or outside the canopies, but the least similarity is found between the largest plot under and the smaller plot outside the canopy (42%). The total number of species is much higher in plots located under ironwood trees. Small plots have about half as many species as large plots, and plots under ironwood trees have roughly twice as many species as those outside their shade (main diagonal in Table 2).

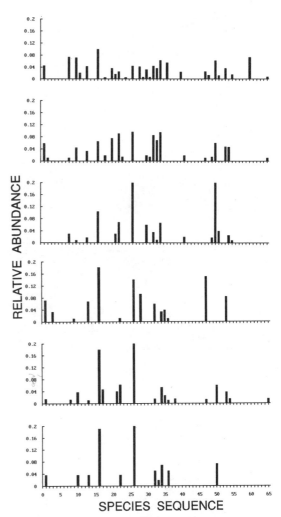

FIG. 4. Typical example of the relative abundance distribution of species on large, medium and small plots respectively, under (top three rows) and outside (lower three rows) ironwood shade at one site (site 1) near Hermosillo, Sonora, México. These are the means for 5 small, 5 medium and 6 large plots under and outside the shade of ironwood trees. Numbers on the abscissa indicate the species as listed in Table 1.

III. Diversity of perennials and importance-value curves

Within each site, abundance varies considerably. In open sites, irrespective of plot size, there is clearly a strong dominance of relatively few species, notably *Encelia farinosa* and *Cenchrus ciliaris* (Fig. 4). As plot size increases, uncommon species are added as one

TABLE 3. Analysis of variance comparing the effect of site (4) and shading (2, under or outside the shade of ironwood trees) on the Shannon-Wiener diversity index using the cover of ironwood trees (or equivalent sampled areas outside the canopy) as a covariate. A regression approach was used wherein all effects are assessed simultaneously, with each effect adjusted for all other effects in the model.

Source of Variation	Sum of Squares	DF	Mean Square	F	P
Cover	34.824	1	34.824	98.38	<.0001
Main effects	32.219	4	8.055	22.75	<.0001
Site	7.006	3	2.335	6.60	<.0001
Shading (under/outside)	25.089	1	25.089	70.87	<.0001
2-way interaction					
Site*Shading	2.644	3	0.881	2.49	.064
Residual	41.771	118	0.354		
Total	110.704	126	0.879		

would expect, but the dominant species keep their relative position. In contrast, for sites under ironwood canopies, relative abundances are more evenly distributed. Species growing under small trees are very similar to those in open sites, but in the medium and large size classes, most species have few individuals with no dominance.

A single value of diversity, measured as heterogeneity on the distribution of species by the Shannon-Wiener index, was computed for each plot from the values of relative abundance. Differences in diversity between the four sites and two treatments of shade were tested using a regression model in an analysis of variance. To adjust for differences in plot sizes, the areas of each plot were used as covariates. The results of the ANOVA are shown in Table 3. A large portion of the variation can be attributed to the area of the plots; when this variation is removed, diversity is mostly affected by the degree of shading of each kind of plot. Species diversity in plots located under ironwood trees is significantly higher than in plots outside its shade. Differences between sites are also highly significant, but the portion of the variation explained by site is much lower than that of shading within sites. No significant interaction between site and shading was found, indicating their independence.

A graphic display of these differences in diversity is depicted for all sites in Figure 5. The curves differ in their slope, which is always steeper, or intercept, with a greater starting diversity for the plots located under the shade of ironwoods. Diversity curves for sites in the small arroyos (2, 4) differ in their intercept, while the curves for sites on the plains are distinctly steeper (1, 3). It is worth considering that ironwoods on the plains resemble more isolated "islands," while in the arroyos many trees cluster forming "big islands" or "large archipelagos."

The sequence of species arranged by their importance values shows dramatic differences between plots located under and outside ironwood canopies (Fig. 6). Without any further refinement of the analysis, it is clear that the rate of change in the value of importance against the species sequence is much larger in plots located outside the shade of ironwoods. However, both curve sets seem to lie between a geometrical series and a lognormal distribution. It is remarkable that despite the differences in plot size, the shape of the curves is very similar within treatments, showing the independence of plot (or tree) size on diversity measures.

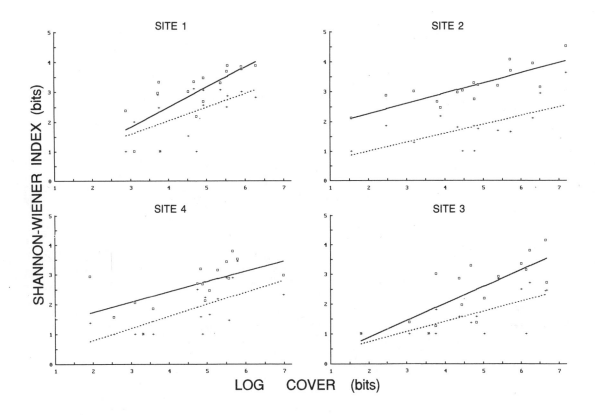

FIG. 5. Shannon-Wiener index of heterogeneity used as a measure of diversity for different sized plots located under (solid line) or outside (dotted line) ironwood trees at four sites near Hermosillo, Sonora, México. Sites 1 and 3 on dry level terrain, sites 2 and 4 along small temporary desert arroyos.

DISCUSSION

Ironwood is one of the most ancient living organisms on earth. This species probably contains the oldest organisms in the Sonoran Desert. Some individuals have been dated by C_{14} as more than 1200 yr old (Ferguson, pers. comm. 1994). In such long-lived species, recruitment events can be far apart, allowing the establishment of individuals in places in which other species, owing to limiting factors, could not be established. Once an ironwood is established, the microclimate and soil properties change directionally, allowing the appearance of other species. Evidence of such discontinuity in recruitment can be inferred from the gaps in the distribution of cover and basal areas of ironwood trees in the four sites studied (see Ogden 1985). The discontinuity is not so apparent

for tree height, but this seeming uniformity could be the result of less variance in height and the way in which the morphology of trees change through time; a rapid increase in height and subsequent spread in cover and basal area.

Shreve (1951) and Shreve and Wiggins (1964) noted that it is not possible to distinguish successional sequences in open communities like the Sonoran Desert. When considering the community as a whole no pattern emerges, species seem to distribute themselves independently from one another in space or time. However, when considering smaller scale communities, tree behavior is analogous to the gap-phase regeneration model described by Hubbell and Foster (1986). Open ground communities are species-poor, and as some protection from the physical or biological environment occurs, a

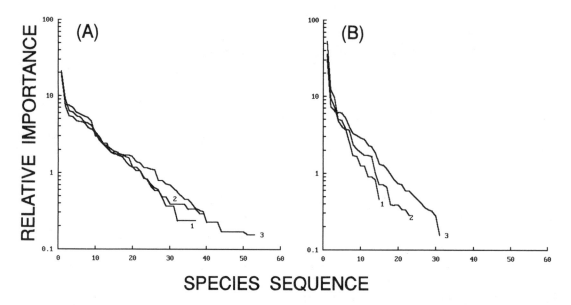

FIG. 6. Dominance-diversity curves in plots of different size (1 = small, 2 = medium, and 3 = large) located under (A), or outside (B) the canopy of ironwood trees. Data pooled from four sites near Hermosillo, Sonora, México.

species accretion process emerges. Young ironwood trees (and probably other trees) modify the environment, protecting other species from the effects of direct irradiance, high temperature, or predation. As trees grow, the physical environment becomes less harsh for many species, creating islands with less irradiance, lower surface temperature, more organic matter and water availability, and probably more protection from large herbivores.

Communities have been described either as collections of independent species or as superorganisms. The idea of the community as an integrated structure has been largely debated (see Richardson 1980). However, in some cases communities can behave as closely tied systems, such as in the case of islands (Williamson 1981), gaps of different size in forests (Brokaw 1990), or the marvelous case of communities in the water collected between the leaves of bromeliads (Laessle 1961, Naeem 1990). The communities under ironwood trees can be seen also as alliances of species in shared conflicts with other species or with the environment (Wilson 1986), or as species sets with specific assembly rules of membership (Cody 1986, 1989). As Wilson (1986) noted in

studying the organization of species alliances, cooperation plays a major role. Cooperation might be a major organizing factor in community assemblage, at a different level than the highly emphasized role given to competition and predation (see Boucher et al. 1982).

Islands of ironwood are more diverse than the rest of the environment and are evidently more productive, appearing as patches of greenery most of the year. Because the productivity of patches under trees of palo verde (*Cercidium microphyllum*) has been shown definitively to be much higher than in exposed areas (Halvorson and Patten 1975, Patten 1978), we assume that a similar situation may occur under ironwood canopies. Interactions are likely to be more numerous under canopies as they not only enhance plant diversity and productivity but support a rich fauna of herbivores and predators (see Turner et al. 1969, Brown et al. 1979) and influence plant fitness (Inouye 1980).

The relationship of perennials under the shade of ironwood trees is probably multifarious and species-dependent. For some vertebrate dispersed species such as *Lycium* spp. and several cacti, the association with ironwood trees might be caused by selective dispersal, and later, better survival in the shade (as found for saguaro; see Olin et al. 1989). However, some bird-dispersed species found under ironwood trees also grow liberally along wire fences dividing cattle fields (Búrquez, unpubl. data). As fences offer protection from herbivory by large mammals, dispersal coupled with the differential predation of seeds, seedlings and juveniles can also account for the association of some plants with ironwood shade (Niering et al. 1963, MacAuliffe 1984).

In the area near Kino Bay, west of our study sites, Vinicio Sosa (pers. comm.) has found that three species of columnar cacti survive as well outside the canopy of mesquite and ironwood as in exposed conditions but protected from predators by a wire cage. Another cause of the association can be the protection from the physical environment, namely protection from high temperature and insolation, by the shade of ironwood as shown for some cacti by Franco and Nobel (1989) and Valiente-Banuet and Ezcurra (1991). Finally, the richer soil under ironwood trees can enhance the survival of seedlings by promoting faster growth under its shade (see García-Moya and McKell 1970, Wallace et al. 1978).

Plant spatial patterning, complexity, and size do affect the species assemblages. This phenomenon is well known for plants (Harper 1977, Grubb 1977, 1986) and animals (MacArthur 1972, Root and Kareiva 1984). Plants under ironwood trees make their living on "archipelagos" of well-protected and well-supplied habitat surrounded by a sea of harsh physical and biological environment. Different areas of cover by ironwood trees reflect variation in space and time available for the establishment of other species. Also, differences relate to the problem of scale, large vs small habitat patches (*sensu* Wiens et al. 1986). The regression approach tested differences between sites, within sites and caused by the size of the plots. Heterogeneity is compounded by the quality of the environment, very much like the differences in nutritional quality between plants as seen by herbivorous insects (Kareiva 1986). The differences in diversity between plots in the plains indicate that even a small degree of protection from the environment

promotes an increase in diversity in a highly rarified and harsh environment. In the arroyo sites, cover is provided by a host of arborescent species in addition to ironwood. Also, cover is much higher than on the plains. The plots outside the shade of ironwood are, in most cases, under the shade of other species such as *Cercidium microphyllum, Coursetia glandulosa, Eysenhardtia orthocarpa, Mimosa laxiflora* and others. The differences in the slope of the curve of diversity vs. plot size reflect more the special role of ironwood for the recruitment and permanence of many perennials (larger rate of change) when compared to other arborescent species in the same area (shallower slope).

The mechanisms that contribute to the maintenance of plant richness have been reviewed by Grubb (1977, 1986). He has addressed this question by investigating the distribution of species and the role played by niche differentiation in maintaining coexistence. Competition and predation models are well documented, but mutualistic interactions are not (see Boucher et al. 1982, Boucher 1985). Ironwood trees provide a continuum of habitat niche variation by altering the irradiance (PER), temperature, nutrient level and microtopography; from areas where young ironwood trees share space with trees and shrubs, casting a diffuse shade that slightly modifies the large-scale habitat, to old ironwood trees that create a distinct microhabitat. Ironwood provides favorable conditions for regeneration to many species with overlapping phenologies, life forms and habitat. In some sense, the establishment of an ironwood tree initiates a process of internal succession or "serule." The plants found growing under ironwood trees comprise organisms with a variety of life history features: different-sized annuals that grow for a short time in the wet seasons of spring or summer, short-lived and long-lived perennials, both annuals and perennials with different generation times, schedules of recruitment, body size, dry-matter allocation, and homeostatic ability. Phenologically, three distinct floras can be associated with the habitat provided by ironwood trees: strict perennials, and summer and spring ephemerals. They partition time and space (see Friedman et al. 1977). Much evidence of temporal separation related mainly to capture of light, water and nutrients is presented by Verosoglu and Fitter (1984), and Rogers and Westman (1979). The species of *Bursera* that occur sympatrically in our study sites show a clear separation in space. *Bursera laxiflora*, the most abundant, grows under and outside the shade of ironwoods, *B. fagaroides* grows only outside its shade, and juveniles of *B. microphylla* were found only under its shade. The latter is the only species of this genus that grows in the central and northern reaches of the Sonoran Desert. In these locations, in the absence of its close relatives, it does not seem to be as closely associated with ironwood.

Our study of perennials only emphasizes coarse dynamics of two major guilds; those associated with ironwood canopies and those that are outside the canopy, but even here a host of approaches to the environment can be seen. Climbers and scandent species use the tree not only for protection from the harsh environment but also for support, short-lived shrubs regenerate under its canopy, and long-lived shrubs and trees are established under the canopy, but later radiate outwards, or thrive after the ironwood tree's death. Chance events like sustained droughts or wet periods are not likely to alter the permanence of the community given the homeostatic effects of long-lived ironwood trees (see Ogden 1985, Davis 1986). The increased diversity and association of species with ironwood in the southern Sonoran Desert is by no means static. Under slightly different environmental conditions, in the Arizona Upland subdivision of the Sonoran Desert, palo verde (*Cercidium microphyllum*) plays a similar role as "nurse plant," while at the very southern end of the desert other trees are likely to share or supplant the protective role of ironwood. Coexistence of perennials under ironwood canopies is probably the result of differences belowground. Ironwood has deep roots, while most of the perennials under its canopy have shallow roots (Búrquez, pers. obs.; Cody 1986). Ironwoods benefit subordinate species by providing rich soil, better water availability and protection from irradiance, while subordinate spe-

cies, by keeping a permanent cover and a shallow root matrix, stabilize the soil and allow water penetration that otherwise would runoff as erosive sheet floods. In certain areas in the central and southern Sonoran Desert, ironwood trees stand in mounds that reflect a higher soil level in the past and a gradual aggregation of soil and organic matter under its crown.

The maintenance of diversity—of life forms, richness of species and other variables of the regeneration niche of many species of ephemerals, shrubs and trees in desert lands—is not a task different from that in the tropical rain forest. As stated by Hubbell and Foster (1986), chance processes are likely to play a major role in determining where a patch of high diversity will be formed. This view is opposed to the traditional belief derived from the competition theory which states that species are the product of competition in stable and saturated systems. For example, the establishment and later presence of mature ironwood trees is homologous to the formation of gaps in the forest. It is impossible to predict where in the desert an ironwood tree will grow. Patches of ironwood are environmentally mediated and depend on rare events of recruitment and survival. However, once established a new "atoll" rises and stays for decades and perhaps centuries. Small changes in the climate could lead to a higher or lower rate of recruitment of ironwood trees, changing the structure of the "archipelago" and affecting the community relations between the abundant subordinate plants and the uncommon ironwood-intolerant species. It is likely that competition and predation are harsh under the canopy of ironwood, and that the interactions increase in number and strength as the diversity of perennials does with "island" size. During years of plenty (rainy and mild), competition can be intense, but in normal years competition could be offset by limitations imposed by the environment (see Wiens et al. 1986). Contrary to current views, competition here is likely to be harsh when water and nutrient availability are maximal, because physical environment restrictions will be released and less space, light and nutrients will be available.

When pooling the species that occur in "archipelagos" of similar-sized ironwood trees, several species cluster together. They occur sparsely when examining the community at a large scale, but are abundant in each patch along gradients of light and nutrients (Tilman 1986). Chance does not seem to play a major role because of the consistency with which plants arrange themselves within patches, but when analyzing similar-sized trees individually, subordinate species seem to occur randomly suggesting limitations to dispersal, available space or resources. Each tree, regardless of size class, differs slightly from all others in the composition and abundance of its associated species.

While ironwood has a positive effect on most associates when considering density or cover under vs. outside the canopy, the underlying species establish complex interactions among themselves. These organisms cannot be considered obligate for they are also found in other microhabitats in the desert: under other large trees, on protected ledges, or along the margins of arroyos. However, it is our experience that they are never as abundant as when they are growing under ironwood trees.

Ironwood populations throughout the Sonoran Desert are currently suffering severe impact from large-scale modifications by man. The historic economic conversion from small-scale farming to extensive cattle-raising has increased overgrazing and favored the clearing of arborescent desert to establish buffel grass pastures. The establishment of artificial grasslands is perhaps the most serious threat to the biological diversity of the Sonoran Desert (Camou 1983, Pérez-López 1992). The most extensive conversion has occurred, and is still occurring, in the southern portions of the Sonoran Desert. In central and southern Sonora, more than 400,000 ha have been cleared already, and more than two million hectares are scheduled for future vegetation conversion. The purpose has been to establish artificial grasslands of the introduced South African buffel-grass (*Cenchrus ciliaris*) as a source of forage for livestock (Johnson and Navarro 1992). If not halted, this practice will perma-

nently change the landscape of the Sonoran Desert and deplete its attendant diversity. We did not expect such a widespread distribution and abundance of this South African grass in a biological reserve, where major land conversion or cattle stocking had not previously occurred. Buffel grass appeared in all size categories at the four sites, irrespective of exposure. Apparently, the *Olneya-Encelia* subdivision of the Sonoran Desert has suffered the most severe impacts from this exotic. Up until now, no formal ecological studies have been published on the impacts of this massive land conversion scheme, or on the effects of this exotic grass on biodiversity. However, our ongoing studies indicate that few woody perennials persist after the establishment of these artificial grasslands because periodic fires rage through the standing grass and combustible detritus destroying the remaining trees.

The presence of ironwood clearly allows most underlying species to survive the otherwise harsh conditions of the desert environment (see Lewis 1973, Davidson and Morton 1981). The disappearance of the sheltered sites provided by dense canopy trees will spell the local extirpation of many species if other suitable microhabitats are lacking.

CONCLUSIONS

Our conclusions are as follows:

1. Ironwood populations studied in the biological reserve appeared to be healthy and stable. From the structure of size classes, recruitment seems to happen in episodes well separated in time. It is unclear the extent to which recently introduced buffel grass might disrupt episodic recruitment in healthy ironwood stands.

2. Despite the obvious historic damage to old trees, resprouting has taken place. Historic pruning did however produce multi-trunk trees. Nevertheless, the general pattern of allometric growth was not affected. Mature trees regained their former morphology in a matter of a few decades. When young, the plants grow more verti-

cally, acquiring a more rotund shape with age.

3. Richness of perennial species under the shade of ironwood trees is about twice that of equivalent areas outside their shade. Of 64 species of perennials identified in the sampling, 52 occur in the shade of ironwood, 31 were found to be positively associated with ironwood, 25 seem to be independent of it, and eight were never found in its shade.

4. The shade of ironwood not only promotes a higher species richness, but also a remarkably greater floristic diversity, or heterogeneity of cover. Most of the variation in diversity from site to site can be explained by the effects of ironwood as a "nurse plant" microhabitat for many perennials. However, a small, but highly significant variation in diversity can also be ascribed to the general environment (macrohabitat) where ironwoods grow.

5. Ironwood plays a major role in promoting increased diversity in the Sonoran Desert. The causes of this seem to be multifarious, but reduced solar radiation below the canopy, increased protection from predation by its armor of spines, better fertility of the soil by the accumulation of litter, and better water availability are likely to be the major contributing factors.

6. Anecdotal evidence and current research indicate that selective cutting (for domestic purposes) and moderate grazing do not destabilize the association. The main threat to the stability of this community is the introduction of buffel grass that rapidly accumulates dead, combustible litter. When burning occurs, ironwood trees burn down entirely and the arborescent desert is replaced by a dry grassland where virtually no recruitment of perennials is possible.

ACKNOWLEDGMENTS

We thank Aidee Miranda, students, and staff of Centro de Ecología at Hermosillo for their help in sampling, as well as Gela Martínez for her comments and constructive discussion. The Government of Sonora kindly provided access to and use of the reserve. Gary Nabhan provided inspiration, criticism, and management of funds; without his efforts this work would not have proceeded. Conservation International (through the Ironwood Alliance) and Consejo Nacional de Ciencia y Tecnología (UNAM 91-0080) provided financial support.

LITERATURE CITED

Alvarez-Buylla, E.R., and M. Martínez-Ramos. 1992. Demography and allometry of *Cecropia obtusifolia*, a Neotropical pioneer tree - an evaluation of the climax-pioneer paradigm for tropical rain forests. Journal of Ecology 80:275-290.

Bartholomew, G.A. 1970. Bare zone between California shrub and grassland communities: the role of animals. Science 170:1210-1212.

Boucher, D.H., S. James and K.H. Keeler. 1982. The ecology of mutualism. Annual Review of Ecology and Systematics 13:315-347.

Boucher, D.H. (ed). 1985. The Biology of Mutualism: Ecology and Evolution. Oxford University Press. Oxford.

Braun-Blanquet, J. 1965. Plant Sociology: The Study of Plant Communities. Hafner. London.

Brokaw, N.V. 1982. The definition of treefall gap and its effect on measures of forest dynamics. Biotropica 14:158-160.

Brokaw, N.V. 1990. Caída de árboles: frecuencia, cronología y consecuencias. Pp. 163-172. *In*: E.G. Leigh Jr, A. S. Rand, and D.M. Wilson (eds), Ecología de un Bosque Tropical: Ciclos Estacionales y Cambios a Largo Plazo.

Smithsonian Tropical Research Institute. Balboa, Panamá.

Brown, J.H., O.J. Reichman and D.H. Davidson. 1979.Granivory in desert ecosystems. Annual Review of Ecology and Systematics 10:201-227.

Búrquez, A., A. Martínez, S. Núñez, T. Quintero and A. Aparício. 1992. Above-ground phytomass of a Sonoran Desert community. American Journal of Botany 79:186.

Camou, E. 1983. Potreros, vegas y mahuechis. Sociedad y ganadería en la Sierra Sonorense. Instituto Sonorense de Cultura. Hermosillo, México.

Cody, M.L. 1986. Structural niches in plant communities. Pp. 381-405. *In*: J. Diamond and T.J. Case (eds), Community Ecology. Harper and Row. New York.

Cody, M.L. 1989. Discussion: Structure and assembly of communities. Pp. 227-241. *In*: J. Roughgarden, R.M. May and S.A. Levin (eds), Perspectives in Ecological Theory. Princeton University Press. Princeton, NJ.

Davidson, D.W. and S.R. Morton. 1981. Competition for dispersal in ant-dispersed plants. Science 213:1259-1261.

Davis, M.B. 1986. Climatic instability, time lags, and community disequilibrium. Pp. 269-284. *In*: J. Diamond and T.J. Case (eds), Community Ecology. Harper and Row. New York.

Diamond, J. 1986. Overview: Laboratory experiments, field experiments, and natural experiments. Pp. 3-22. *In*: J. Diamond and T.J. Case (eds), Community Ecology. Harper and Row. New York.

Dirzo, R., C.C. Horvitz, H. Quevedo and M.A. López. 1992. The effects of gap size and age on the understorey herb community of a tropical Mexican rain forest. Journal of Ecology 80:809-822.

Felger, R.S. and M.B. Moser. 1985. People of the Desert and the Sea: Ethnobotany of the Seri Indians. Univerity of Arizona Press. Tucson, AZ.

Franco, A.C. and P.S. Nobel. 1989. Effects of nurse plants on the microhabitat and growth of cacti. Journal of Ecology 77:870-886.

Friedman, J., G. Orshan and Y. Ziger-Cfir. 1977. Supression of annuals by *Artemisia herba-alba* in the Negev Desert of Israel. Journal of Ecology 65:413-426.

García-Moya, E. and M.C. McKell. 1970. Contributionof shrubs in the economy of a desert wash plant community. Ecology 51:81-88.

Grubb, P.J. 1977. The maintenance of species-richness in plant communities: the importance of the regeneration niche. Biological Reviews 52:107-145.

Grubb, P.J. 1986. Problems posed by sparse and patchily distributed species in species-rich plant communities. Pp. 207-227. *In*: J. Diamond and T.J. Case (eds), Community Ecology. Harper and Row. New York.

Halvorson, W.L. and D.T. Patten. 1975. Productivity and flowering of winter ephemerals in relation to Sonoran Desert shrubs. American Midland Naturalist 93:311-319.

Harper, J.L. 1977. Population Biology of Plants. Academic Press. London.

Hastings, J.R., R.M. Turner and D.K. Warren. 1972. An atlas of some plant distributions in the Sonoran Desert. Technical Reports on the Meteorology and Climatology of Arid Regions 21. University of Arizona Institute of Atmospheric Physics, Tucson.

Hubbell, S.P. and R.B. Foster. 1985. Canopy gaps and the dynamics of a Neotropical forest. Pp. 77-96. *In*: M.J. Crawley (ed), Plant Ecology. Blackwell. Oxford.

Hubbell, S.P. and R.B. Foster. 1986. Biology, chance, and history and the structure of tropical rain forest tree communities. Pp. 314-329. *In*: J. Diamond and T.J. Case (eds), Community Ecology.

Harper and Row. New York.

Inouye, R.S. 1980. Density dependent germination response by seeds of desert annuals. Oecologia 46:235-238.

Johnson, D. and A. Navarro. 1992. Zacate buffel y biodiversidad en el Desierto Sonorense. Pp. 117-122. *In*: J.L. Moreno (ed), Ecología, Recursos Naturales y Medio ambiente en Sonora. SIUE/Colegio de Sonora. Hermosillo, México.

Kareiva, P. 1986. Patchiness, dispersal, and species interactions: consequences for communities of herbivorous insects. Pp. 192-206. *In*: J. Diamond and T.J. Case (eds), Community Ecology. Harper and Row. New York.

Laessle, A.M. 1961. A micro-limnological study of Jamaican bromeliads. Ecology 42:499-517.

Lewis, D.H. 1973. The relevance of symbiosis to taxonomy and ecology, with particular reference to mutualistic symbioses and the exploitation of marginal habitats. Pp. 151-172. *In*: V.H. Heywood (ed), Taxonomy and Ecology. Academic Press. London.

MacArthur, R.H. 1972. Geographical Ecology. Harperand Row. New York.

McAuliffe, J.R. 1984. Prey refugia and the distribution of two Sonoran desert cacti. Oecologia 65:82-85.

Mueller-Dumbois, D. and H. Ellenberg. 1974. Aims and Methods of Vegetation Ecology. John Wiley and Sons. New York.

Naeem, S. 1990. Resource heterogeneity and community structure: A case study in *Heliconia imbricata* Phytoelmata. Oecologia 84:29-38.

Niering, W.A., R.H. Whittaker and C.H. Lowe. 1963. The saguaro: A population in relation to environment. Science 142:15-23.

Ogden, J. 1985. Past, present and future: Studies on the population dynamics of some long-lived trees. Pp. 3-16. *In*: J. White (ed), Studies on Plant Demography: A Festschrift for John L.

Harper. Academic Press. London.

Olin, G., S.M. Alcorn and J.M. Alcorn. 1989. Dispersal of viable saguaro seeds by white-winged doves (*Zenaida asiatica*). Southwestern Naturalist 34:282-284.

Patten, D.T. 1978. Productivity and production efficiency of an Upper Sonoran Desert ephemeral community. American Journal of Botany 65:891-895.

Peet, R.K. 1974. The measurement of species diversity. Annual Review of Ecology and Systematics 5:285-307.

Pérez-López, E.P. 1992. La ganadería bovina Sonorense: cambios productivos y deterioro del medio ambiente. Pp. 197-216. *In:* J.L. Moreno (ed), Ecología, Recursos Naturales y Medio Ambiente en Sonora. SIUE/Colegio de Sonora. Hermosillo, México.

Richardson, J.L. 1980. The organismic community: resilience of an embattled ecological concept. BioScience 30:465-471.

Rogers, R.W. and W.E. Westman. 1979. Niche differentiation and maintenace of genetic identity in cohabiting *Eucalyptus* species. Australian Journal of Ecology 4:429-439.

Root, R.B. and P. Kareiva. 1984. The search for resources by cabbage butterflies (*Pieris rapae*): Ecological consequences and adaptive significance of Markovian movement in a patchy environment. Ecology 65:147-165.

Shreve, F. 1951. Vegetation of the Sonoran Desert. Carnegie Institution of Washington, Publ. 591.

Shreve, F. and I.L. Wiggins 1964. Vegetation and flora of the Sonoran Desert. Stanford University Press. Stanford, CA.

Steenbergh, W.F. and C.H. Lowe. 1977. Ecology of the saguaro: II. Reproduction, germination, establishment, growth, and survival of the young plant. National Park Service Scientific Monograph Ser. 17. Washington, DC.

Suzán, H., G.P. Nabhan, and D.T. Patten. In press.

Nurse plant and floral biology of a rare night-blooming cereus, *Peniocereus striatus* (Brandegee) Buxbaum. Conservation Biology.

Tilman, D. 1986. Evolution and differentiation in terrestrial plant communities: The importance of the soil resource:light gradient. Pp. 359-380. *In*: J. Diamond and T.J. Case (eds), Community Ecology. Harper and Row. New York.

Turner, R.M., S.M. Alcorn and G. Olin. 1969. Mortality of transplanted saguaro seedlings. Ecology 50:835-844.

Turner, R.M., S.M. Alcorn, G. Olin and J.A. Booth. 1966. The influence of shade, soil, and water on saguaro seedling establishment. Botanical Gazette 127:95-102.

Valiente-Banuet, A. and E. Ezcurra. 1991. Shade as a cause of the association between the cactus *Neobuxbaumia tetetzo* and the nurse plant *Mimosa luisiana* in the Tehuacán Valley, México. Journal of Ecology 79:961-971.

Verosoglu, D.S. and A.H. Fitter. 1984. Spatial and temporal patterns of growth and nutrient uptake of five co-existing grasses. Journal of Ecology 72:259-272.

Wallace, A., E.M. Romney, G.E. Kleinkopf, and M. Soufi. 1978. Uptake of mineral forms of nitrogen by desert plants. Pp. 130-151. *In:* West and J.J. Skujins (eds.) Nitrogen in Desert Ecosystems. Dowden, Hutchinson and Ross, Inc. Stroudsburg, PA.

Wiens, J.A., J.F. Addicot, T.J. Case and J. Diamond. 1986. Overview: The importance of spatial and temporal scale in ecological investigations. Pp. 145-153. *In:* J. Diamond and T.J. Case (eds), Community Ecology. Harper and Row. New York.

Williamson, M. 1981. Island Populations. Oxford University Press. Oxford.

Wilson, D.S. 1986. Adaptive indirect effects. Pp. 437-444. *In:* J. Diamond and T.J. Case (eds), Community Ecology. Harper and Row. New York.

A. Búrquez and M. A. Quintana
Centro de Ecología
Universidad Nacional Autónoma de México
Apartado Postal 1354
Hermosillo, Sonora 83000
México

THE INFLUENCES OF IRONWOOD AS A HABITAT MODIFIER SPECIES: A CASE STUDY ON THE SONORAN DESERT COAST OF THE SEA OF CORTEZ

Joshua J. Tewksbury and Christian A. Petrovich*

ABSTRACT

This report presents an analysis of the patterns of diversity associated with the canopies of *Olneya tesota* (Gray), desert ironwood, in the Central Gulf Coast subregion of the Sonoran Desert. The species richness and abundance of all perennial vegetation under ironwood was compared with that of random samples in the same habitats. Under the ironwood canopy, species richness was 36% greater and abundance was 46% greater than random samples in the surrounding environment. Growth forms showing the greatest increases in species richness and abundance under ironwood canopies include: epiphytes, large cacti, vines, large shrubs, small perennials, and medium-sized shrubs, in descending order.

The effects of ironwood were much larger in areas without ephemeral watercourses, suggesting that the conditions created by ironwood are similar to those created by xeroriparian areas. In riparian habitats, ironwood increased abundance by 19% and species richness by 13%. In nonriparian habitats, ironwood increased abundance by 88% and species richness by 64%. The increased structural heterogeneity provided by both ironwood itself and the perennial plants it supports may increase faunal diversity as well. The results of our study demonstrate the ecological importance of ironwood to the biodiversity of one subregion of the desert coastlands along the Sea of Cortez.

RESÚMEN

Este reporte presenta un análisis de los patrones de diversidad asociados con los doseles de *Olneya tesota* (Gray), palo fierro, en la subregión de la Costa del Golfo Central del Desierto Sonorense. La riqueza de especies y la abundancia de la vegetación perenne creciendo bajo el dosel del palo fierro fueron comparadas con áreas seleccionados al azar dentro del mismo hábitat. Bajo el dosel del palo fierro, la riqueza de especies era 36% mayor, y la abundancia era 46% mayor que la de otras muestras en el ambiente local. Los tipos de plantas que mostraron la mayor riqueza de especies y abundancia en número de individuos bajo el dosél del palo fierro incluyen: epífitas, cactus grandes, lianas, arbustos grandes, perrenes pequeñas, y arbustos medianos, en un orden descendiente.

    Los efectos del palo fierro fueron mucho más intenso en las áreas fuera de arroyos, sugiriendo que las condiciones creadas por el palo fierro son parecidas a aquellas creadas por las áreas ribereñas. En los hábitats

---

*This paper was equally coauthored.

ribereños, el palo fierro incrementó la abundancia de individuos un 19% y la riqueza de especies un 13%, mientras que en los hábitats no ribereños, el palo fierro aumentó la abundancia por 88%, y la riqueza de especies un 64%. Las evidencias preliminares indican que el incremento de la heterogeneidad estructural introducida al ecosistema, tanto por el palo fierro mismo, como por la diversidad de plantas perennes asociadas a la especie, también juegan un papel importante en incrementar la diversidad de la fauna. Los resultados de éste estudio demuestran la importancia ecológica del palo fierro para la biodiversidad de la subregión del desierto costeño a lo largo del Mar de Cortez.

INTRODUCTION

The Sonoran Desert is the most structurally diverse arid land ecosystem in North America (Turner and Brown 1982). Within this system, the interactions taking place between plants, animals, and the physical environment form a complex, highly integrated web of dependencies and associations that have evolved since the landscape was covered with junipers, oaks, and pines 9,000 years before the present (Axelrod 1979). The patterns of diversity found in the Sonoran Desert today reveal a mosaic of the differential influences imparted by the limiting factors affecting biodiversity, and the high degree of complexity found in this living system.

This study assesses the influence of one prominent Sonoran Desert species, desert ironwood, on patterns of perennial plant diversity, illuminating the role of desert ironwood in shaping the landscape which it occupies. By way of illustration, it is useful to consider Ludwig von Bertalanffy's generalized sketch of how living systems effect self-integration as they ascend in complexity (Davidson 1983). As living systems become more complex, the parts become more dependant on the whole, and certain parts emerge that play leading roles in determining the behavior of the system. The ecological integrity of the highly complex Sonoran Desert ecosystem is, thus, maintained through a highly integrated web of interactions between component species and their overlapping environments (King 1993, Regier 1993). Still, certain species have stronger, more abundant and more integrated interactions than others, thus emerging as leading parts which greatly affect the behav-

ior of the system (Davidson 1983). This study attempts to quantify the role of ironwood as a leading part in a natural system, a species with strong interactions that greatly affect the composition of perennial plant communities in the Sonoran Desert.

Ironwood is a prominent Sonoran Desert legume with both nitrogen fixing and evergreen qualities. In the last 60 years, many researchers and naturalists have made qualitative observations regarding the clustering of other plants under ironwood canopies. As early as 1951, Forest Shreve reported such nonrandom distributions, and later, these were substantiated by Felger (1966) and McAuliffe (1984). Based on these qualitative assessments, we hypothesized and quantitatively tested whether or not there is an increase in the species richness and abundance of perennial plants under ironwood canopies.

Endemic to the Sonoran Desert, ironwood is most abundant on the Gulf Coast and on the Plains of Sonora (Shreve 1951). Ironwood may grow to heights exceeding fifteen meters and under favorable conditions can achieve a life-span exceeding 800 years (Humberto Suzán, pers. comm.; Wes Ferguson, unpubl.), long outliving all other desert trees. Although found in a wide variety of habitats, ironwood is commonly considered a facultative xeroriparian species (Turner and Brown 1982) as it attains its maximum height and densities along intermittent and ephemeral watercourses (Shreve 1951, Wiggins 1980).

Qualitative studies of other desert trees have found that the shade they provide causes an increase in the number of cacti under their canopies (Turner et al.

1966, McAuliffe 1984, Hutto et al. 1986). Large desert trees have also been studied with relation to their effects on available soil moisture (Shreve 1931, Patten 1978). Results from these studies show associated plants increasing in both plant productivity and diversity under the canopies of the large trees (Mares et al. 1977, Patten 1978). This increase may be due to the tree's shade augmenting soil moisture available to underlying plants. Forest Shreve (1951) observed that the clumping of other plants under desert trees becomes more dense and more diverse in the southern parts of the Sonoran Desert, where the water-limiting conditions of exposed soils are more severe.

We focused our research on the Central Gulf Coast subregion of the Sonoran Desert. This is a dry subregion, receiving an average of 12.7 cm of precipitation per year. Despite its coastline, the vegetation found here is distinctly continental in character (Shreve 1951, Turner and Brown 1982). The central question of our study was, how do ironwood trees affect the species richness, abundance, and size of perennial vegetation in the Gulf Coast of the Sonoran Desert? A secondary pursuit was for preliminary evidence of ironwood microhabitat use by birds, mammals, and reptiles.

METHODS

Study Sites

Data were collected between June 15 and August 15, 1993. Eight of the 10 sites used were located south of Puerto Libertad and north of Bahía Kino, all within 15 km from the coast of the Sea of Cortez in Sonora, México (Fig. 1 and Table 1). Two sites were located on Tiburón Island, a large island just off the coast at Punta Chueca. The 10 sites were located in a variety of vegetative associations within the Central Gulf Coast region and comprised a cross-section of habitat types within which ironwood can be found.

The 10 1-ha sites were selected to represent the diverse range of topography, vegetative communities, watercourses, and soil types found within the Central Gulf Coast Subregion (Table 1; see Appendix 1 for thorough site descriptions). Because of site variation, our results represent both the effects of ironwood in different habitat types and the overall effect of ironwood in this subregion. One-ha sites were chosen to include a minimum of seven ironwood trees. Each ironwood counted was at least 1.5 meters tall and possessed a definite canopy.

Square 1-ha sites were used where ironwoods were evenly distributed throughout the landscape. These sites were marked using a measured rope and compass. Linear 1-ha sites were used where ironwoods were distributed along a wash. These were marked by walking the length of the site on the center of the wash and marking the sides a certain distance from the center.

Survey Methods

Within a study site, each ironwood was counted and a defined area of 128 m² around it was surveyed for associated perennial plant species richness and abundance. This method was adapted from McAuliffe (1990).

TABLE 1. Study site locations and general landscape character.

#	Name	Latitude	Longitude	Site Character
1	Adobe	28° 55' N	112° 02' W	coastal bajada
2	Tortilla	28° 54' N	111° 51' W	inland plain
3	Hummer	28° 59' N	112° 04' W	deep wash
4	Bee-tongue	29° 33' N	112° 25' W	coastal bajada
5	Bosque	29° 35' N	112° 22' W	large wash
6	Highland	29° 37' N	112° 23' W	upland bajada
7	Dense	29° 52' N	112° 37' W	small, inland wash
8	Millipede	29° 54' N	112° 35' W	cutbank wash
9	Dragonfly	28° 49' N	112° 25' W	low terrace, old floodplain
10	Vista	28° 48' N	112° 25' W	terrace

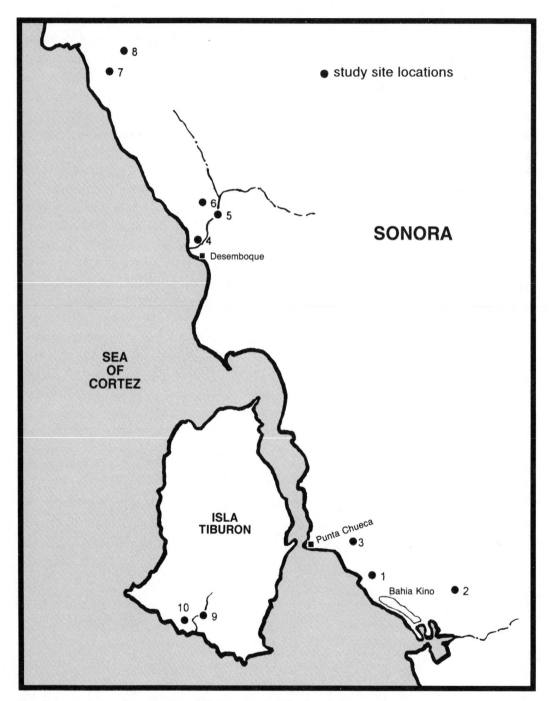

FIG. 1. Study site locations. See Appendix I for detailed site descriptions.

Randomly placed control plots of equal size and dimensions were also surveyed in the same manner. The number of random plots equaled the number of ironwood plots surveyed on each study site.

Each ironwood was measured using a standard 30 m tape. The height of each tree was recorded, and the size of the canopy (lateral distance from the center of the trunk) was recorded in the cardinal directions. The four numbers were averaged to produce an average canopy radius. The study circle covering 128 m^2 in area with its center at the trunk (or center point of multiple trunks) was marked. These circular plots were divided into two separate parts: the canopy, delineated as the area receiving some overhead cover from the ring of ironwood branches, and the outer ring, delineated as the area beyond the canopy but still within the 128 m^2 circle. This canopy/outer circle distinction was made to determine the effect of ironwood under its canopy and to see if the effect extended beyond the canopy. All circular plots were surveyed using a marked rope.

All perennial plants found in the plot were counted and recorded as being in the canopy plot or in the outer ring plot. Perennial grasses were not included in the study (see monograph plant list for species encountered in this study). Counts were done if there were fewer than one hundred individuals of a species; estimates derived from counts in several 1 m^2 areas were used if the species was more abundant. In order to estimate the effect of ironwood on the size of individuals within a species, an average cover class category was ascribed to each species in each study plot.

When two ironwood canopies overlapped, the trees were considered to represent one continuous canopy from the perspective of the flora found beneath, and the two trees were surveyed as one. This situation occurred only four times in a total sample size of 144 canopy survey plots. When the outer ring overlapped the canopy of a neighboring ironwood, the outer ring of the former ironwood was omitted and only the canopy was surveyed. This was done so that the effect of ironwood beyond its canopy would not be confused by the effect of the neighboring ironwood's canopy. Of the 144 study ironwoods, 72 outer rings were surveyed.

Center points for randomly located control plots were selected using a frisbee. The frisbee was thrown with eyes closed while spinning in place. As long as the frisbee landed inside the 1-ha study site, and not in the center of a lifeless dry watercourse, it was used for the random survey plot.

Data for the random plots were taken in exactly the same manner as they were taken for the ironwood plots. "Canopy area" for random plots was determined by the average canopy area for all the ironwoods surveyed in the study site. In this way, data from a random area of equal size was directly compared with the data from the canopies of the ironwood at that study site.

When the frisbee landed so that a randomly located control plot included the canopy and/or the trunk of an ironwood, the plot was surveyed as usual, on the basis that the general habitat included ironwood trees and the controls were designed to be a representation of the entire general habitat. This was not a common occurrence, out of 143 random canopy-sized survey plots, nine were influenced by ironwood (6.4%) and out of 71 outer rings, 14 had some influence of ironwood (18.2%).

Growth Form Classification

All plants surveyed were classified into their respective growth forms using categories modified from those of Felger (1966). The following categories were used:

Arborescents: those plants generally attaining 3.5 m or more in height, having a discernable canopy and possessing one to few trunks.

Large shrubs: entirely woody plants with heights between 1.5 and 3.5 m. Most of the thorn bearing plants found in our study, except for three prominent tree species, were of this growth form.

Medium-sized shrubs: this highly variable growth form is comprised of those plants usually between 0.75 and 1.5

m in height, ranging from densely branched shrubs such as *Simmondsia chinensis* to smaller plants such as *Encelia farinosa*.

Small perennials: all perennial vegetation generally less than 0.5 m in height and having a definite non-woody character. This growth form includes all the suffrutescents and herbaceous perennials found in our study sites.

Large cacti: this growth form consists of four species found on our study sites: *Pachycereus pringlei*, *Carnegiea gigantea*, *Stenocereus thurberi* and *Lophocereus schottii*.

Medium-sized cacti: this class is composed of the medium-sized cacti including *Opuntia* and *Ferocactus*.

Small cacti: this growth form is composed of *Mammillaria* and *Echinocereus*.

Vines: those plants with tendrils and/or those plants that climb into other plants for structural support.

Epiphytes: plants that grow on other plants. The only two epiphytes found in this study are parasitic plants, *Phoradendron californicum* and *Struthanthus palmeri*.

Animal Observations

Preliminary observational data were recorded on other aspects of ironwood ecology. Bird nest frequencies were determined for nine of the ten 1-ha sites by looking in all the trees and shrubs on the site, counting each nest found, and recording the host plant species. Nests found in cacti were not included in our survey because of the specificity of cactus nesting birds. In addition, any other animal activity associated with ironwood was recorded. These activities included bedding, chew marks on ironwood branches, and direct observations of vertebrate activities.

Data Analysis

Mean plant species richness, abundances per plot and standard errors were determined using the Quattro Pro spreadsheet program. Differences in plant species richness and abundances between ironwood and random plots were analyzed using standard two-tailed, paired t-tests, at the 0.05 level of significance. Species diversity indices were determined using the Shannon-Weaver diversity index, and from that the Hill's N1 number (representing the number of abundant species) was determined (Ludwig and Reynolds 1988). Bird nest preferences were analyzed using a chi-square test.

RESULTS

Overall, the effect of ironwood on the species richness and abundance of perennial plants is concentrated under the canopy (Figs. 2 and 3). The effect did not extend beyond the canopy. In light of this trend, we discuss outer circle results only when significant differences were found.

There was a significant increase in both overall species richness (t=5.04, t>1.960; Fig. 2) and abundance (t=2.96, t>2.000; Fig. 3) of the perennial vegetation under the canopy of ironwood. There was a 36% overall increase in species richness of perennial vegetation under the canopy of ironwood as compared to the random plots of equal size (an average of 6.3 species per ironwood plot, 4.7 per canopy random plot). The total increase in the abundance of perennial vegetation in the same comparison was 46% (an average of 19.1 individuals in the ironwood canopy plots and 13.0 in the random plots).

This total ironwood effect on abundance and species richness differed enormously between non-xeroriparian and xeroriparian habitats. Ironwood increased the abundance of perennial plants by 19% in riparian habitats, but by 88% in nonriparian habitats. Additionally, ironwood increased species richness by 13% in riparian habitats, but by 64% in nonriparian habitats. Ironwood clearly has its greatest habitat-modi-

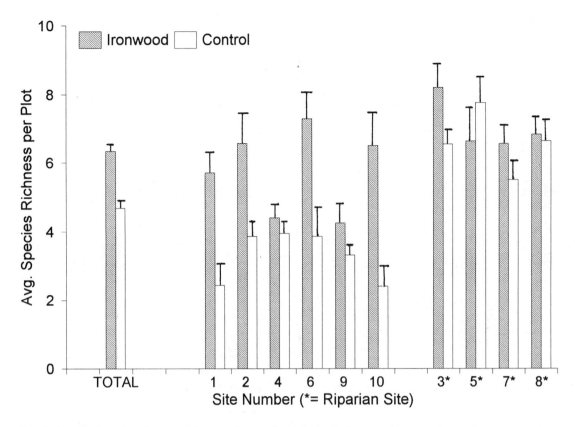

FIG. 2. Distribution of total perennial vegetation species richness for ironwood canopy plots and control canopy plots at each site and for the entire study (total includes all 10 sites). Total N=144 and 143 for ironwood and control canopy plots, respectively. Standard error is indicated.

fying effect in the drier, nonriparian habitat (Fig. 4).

We encountered a statistically significant increase in species richness and abundance under ironwood canopies among the following growth forms: large shrubs, large cacti, small perennials, vines, epiphytes and medium shrubs (Figs. 5 and 6). Of all the growth forms, large shrubs and large cacti showed the most consistent and definite increase in both species richness and abundance under the ironwood canopy (Figs. 7-10). Table 2 provides a list of those species with the largest difference in abundance under ironwood canopies as compared to the general habitat.

Significant differences in the average plant size within a species under ironwood vs. the general habitat were seen in the following growth forms: arborescents, small perennials, large cacti, and medium cacti (Fig. 11).

Growth Forms

1. Arborescents

In contrast to the general trends, arborescent vegetation showed a 43% decrease in species richness under the canopy of ironwood (t=2.35, t>1.96). Abundance trends are similar, but the decrease in abundance under ironwood was not statistically valid (only 11%; t=-1.18, t>1.96). The presence of *Cercidium microphyllum* is probably responsible for this decrease in species richness and abundance, as almost 50% of all the trees found in our study were *C. microphyllum*, and it is found much less often under ironwood than in the controls (0.07 trees per ironwood canopy plot and 0.12 in the control plots). This trend may represent competition between two legume trees. The average size of trees found under the

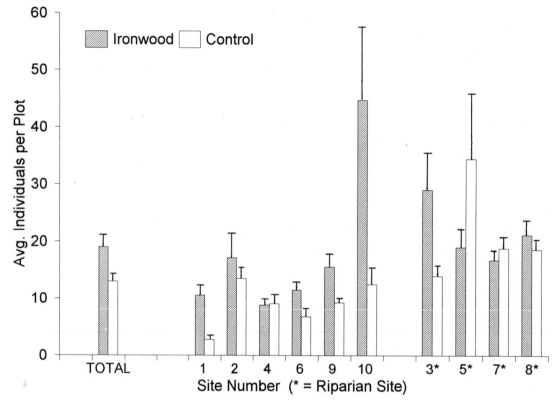

FIG 3. Distribution of total perennial vegetation abundance for ironwood canopy plots and control canopy plots at each site and for the entire study (total includes all 10 sites). Total N=144 and 143 for ironwood and control canopy plots, respectively. Standard error is indicated.

canopy of ironwood was 21% smaller than controls, further illustrating possible competition, but also pointing to the larger number of arborescent seedlings found in the shelter of the ironwood canopy.

2. Large shrubs

Large shrubs increased both in species richness (t=4.40, t>1.96) and abundance (t=3.58, t>1.96) under the ironwood canopy. This trend was found at almost every site (Figs. 7 and 8). There was a 50% increase in species richness in the ironwood canopy plots (1.7 species in ironwood plots to 1.1 species in random plots) and a 60% increase in abundance (3.1 individuals in ironwood plots to 2.0 individuals in random plots). Under ironwood, large shrubs showed a higher N1 number on Hill's diversity index (N1=7.2) than in the controls (N1=5.8) (Table 3). The large N1 number under ironwood was probably influenced by the abundance of *Lycium*

andersonii throughout the study, which experienced a strong increase under ironwood. Other common species, such as *Colubrina glabra* and *Zizyphus obtusifolia*, showed even stronger increases in numbers under ironwood (Table 2). No large shrubs species decreased in population size under ironwood, although two of the most abundant large shrubs, *Larrea tridentata* and *Jatropha cuneata*, remained unaffected. Average size of large shrubs dropped 10% under the canopies of ironwood.

Following overall trends, no changes in the abundance or species richness of large shrubs occurred in the outer ring plots. Two riparian sites, #7 and #8, showed exceptions, where *Lycium andersonii* and *Larrea tridentata* decreased in population size around ironwood.

3. Medium-sized shrubs

Although the overall increase in species richness was not as great as for large shrubs, we found a 28% difference in medium-sized shrub species richness under ironwood (t=2.53, t>1.96), from 1.1 species in control plots to 1.5 species under ironwood. The N1 diversity index increased as well, from 6.3 in controls to 6.9 under ironwood (Table 3). These increases in species richness were attributed mostly to sites #1 and #6, where the effect of ironwood canopies was dramatic. The heightened species richness of medium-sized shrubs was not matched by changes in the growth form's abundance, which remained unaffected.

4. Small perennials

The species richness of small perennials showed an overall increase under ironwood of 32% (t=3.04, t>1.96), from 1.3 species per control plot to 1.8 species per ironwood plot. The N1 diversity index indicates a much higher number of abundant small perennials growing in the control plots (N1=10.17) than under ironwood canopies (N1=8.23) (Table 3). As a result, most of the increase in diversity under ironwood was due to the less abundant, perhaps more ecologically restricted, small perennials. Overall abundance values showed a 62% increase in small perennials under the canopy of ironwood (t=1.95, t>1.96) with an average of 8.3 individuals per ironwood plot compared to an average of 5.1 individuals in the control plots. Small perennials were the

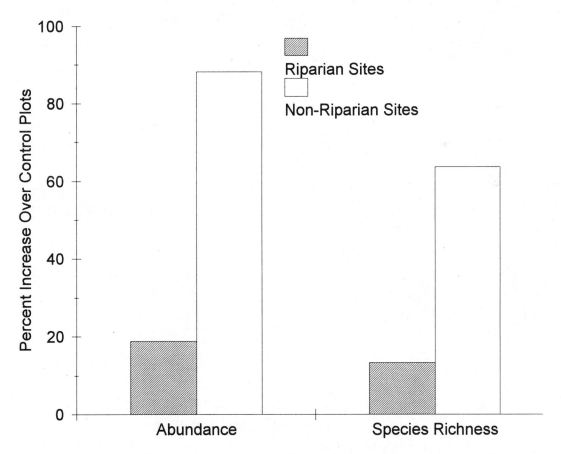

FIG 4. Percentage increase in the abundance and species richness of riparian sites over nonriparian sites.

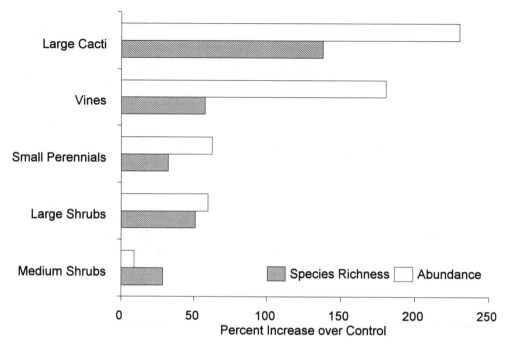

FIG 5. Percentage increase of species richness and abundance in perennial plant life by growth form in ironwood canopy plots over random (control) canopy plots. N=144 for canopy plots.

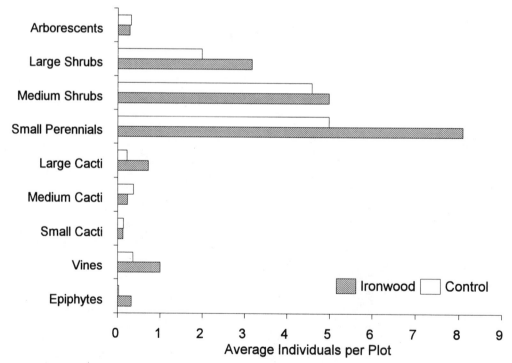

FIG 6. Distribution of perennial plant life by growth form in ironwood canopy plots and random (control) canopy plots. N=144 for canopy plots.

only non-succulent growth form to show an increase in average canopy size under ironwood (Fig. 11), up 21% over the control value of 0.37 m^2.

Abutilon californicum appeared in remarkable numbers under ironwood and was very limited in numbers outside of the canopy (Table 2). This trend was consistent at every site where *A. californicum* was found and was one of the strongest across-the-board increases in population size under ironwood. We also found *Lyrocarpa coulteri* to increase dramatically in numbers under the canopy of ironwood. *Spharalcea ambigua* and *Eriogonum trichopes* decreased in numbers under ironwood.

5. Large cacti

The relationship between large cacti and arborescents in the Sonoran Desert has been studied most notably by McAuliffe (1984), who found a definite, non-random pattern of growth for these cacti in relation to desert trees and shrubs. Our findings were similar, with a large increase in species richness, up 138% (t=4.00, t>1.96), and abundance, up 230% (t=4.08, t>1.96) under the canopy of ironwood.

The species richness of large cacti under ironwood was higher than in controls in nearly all of the study sites (Fig. 9). There was an overall average of 0.5 species per plot under ironwood and only 0.2 species per random plot (Figs. 5 and 9). This was matched with an increase in the abundance of most of the cacti of this growth form (Figs. 5, 6 and 10). *Pachycereus pringlei*, *Carnegiea gigantea* and *Lophocereus schottii* all showed definite population increases under ironwood (Table 2). *Lophocereus schottii*, a species encountered often throughout our study, appeared under ironwood four times as often as in the random plots of equal size. The increase in large cacti abundance under ironwood seems to be most apparent in areas of less dense vegetation with higher diversity of cacti species (Fig. 9). The average size of large cacti individuals also increased dramatically under ironwood canopies (Fig. 11), showing an

87% increase in canopy size (an average of 0.8 m^2 in controls and 1.5 m^2 under ironwood canopies).

6. Medium-sized cacti

Opuntia and *Ferocactus* seem to show little requirement for the protected microclimate generated by ironwood, as both the average species richness and abundance showed no significant change in numbers between the two plot types. However, medium-sized cacti showed a large increase in size under the canopies of ironwood, averaging 0.81 m^2 under ironwoods and only 0.46 m^2 in control plots (Fig. 11).

7. Small cacti

The frequency of small cacti was very low, with an average abundance of 0.13 individuals in control plots vs. 0.12 in ironwood canopy plots, a total population size of only 36 individuals for the entire growth form; a population too small for meaningful conclusions.

8. Epiphytes

As a growth form requiring another plant upon which to grow, there was an 840% increase of epiphyte abundance in ironwood canopies over the control plots (t=3.31, t>1.96). We found only two species of epiphytes in our study, both of them parasitic.

9. Vines

Vines benefit greatly from the presence of a structure to climb on, although not all vines require one. *Phaseolus filiformis*, for example, was often found growing on the ground without any support. Still, with the assistance of a tree in each ironwood canopy plot, vines increased in abundance by 180% over controls (t=3.73, t>1.96). There was an average of 1.3 vines per ironwood plot and 0.4 vines per control plot. The species richness of vines increased as well, by 83% (t=3.21, t>1.96). There were 0.5 species per ironwood plot as compared to 0.3 species per control plot.

TABLE 2. Per plot frequencies of perennial vegetation with the largest frequency differences between the iron-wood canopy plots and the equal-sized random (control) plots. Total N=144 and 143 for ironwood and control canopy plots, respectively.

A. Increase in abundance under ironwood vs. control plots

Species	Per Plot Frequency			Total Number	
	Ironwood	Control	% Up	Ironwood	Control
ARBORESCENTS					
Prosopis glandulosa	0.08	0.07	19%	12	10
LARGE SHRUBS					
Lycium andersonii	1.07	0.46	135%	154	65
Colubrina glabra	0.31	0.08	297%	44	11
Jatropha cinerea	0.31	0.18	75%	44	25
Zizyphus obtusifolia	0.12	0.03	322%	17	4
Atamisquea emarginata	0.11	0.01	1489%	16	1
Justicia californica	0.07	0.04	99%	10	5
MEDIUM-SIZED SHRUBS					
Encelia farinosa	2.19	1.38	59%	315	197
Ambrosia deltoidea	0.71	0.50	41%	102	72
Simmondsia chinensis	0.44	0.20	123%	63	28
Lippia palmeri	0.13	0.10	35%	19	14
Stegnosperma halmifolium	0.13	0.01	843%	19	2
Melochia tomentosa	0.10	0.06	54%	14	9
Krameria grayi	0.09	0.08	17%	13	11
Hyptis emoryi	0.06	0.04	49%	9	6
Solanum hindsianum	0.05	0.03	74%	7	4
Viscainoa geniculata	0.05	0.03	74%	7	4
SMALL PERENNIALS					
Abutilon californicum	3.28	0.52	533%	472	74
Lyrocarpa coulteri	1.19	0.55	116%	172	79
Euphorbia xantii	0.89	0.73	21%	128	105
Horsfordia newberryi	0.43	0.16	168%	62	23
Hibiscus denudatus	0.38	0.18	110%	55	26
Ditaxis lanceolata	0.35	0.17	107%	50	24
Ambrosia ambrosioides	0.23	0.18	31%	33	25
Trixis californica	0.19	0.06	248%	28	8
Fagonia californica	0.19	0.08	144%	27	11
Ruellia californica	0.06	0.02	198%	9	3
Porophyllum gracile	0.06	0.01	347%	9	2
LARGE CACTI					
Lophocereus schottii	0.44	0.11	297%	64	16
Carnegiea gigantea	0.15	0.06	173%	22	8
Pachycereus pringlei	0.10	0.01	645%	15	2
MEDIUM-SIZED CACTI					
Opuntia fulgida	0.12	0.08	41%	17	12

TABLE 2. *continued*

VINES					
Cardiospermum corindum	0.38	0.11	258%	54	15
Jacquemontia abutiloides	0.22	0.03	670%	31	4
Phaseolus filiformis	0.17	0.08	126%	25	11
Ibervillea sonorae	0.16	0.07	128%	23	10
EPIPHYTES					
Phoradendron californicum	0.31	0.03	992%	44	4

B. Decrease in abundance under ironwood.

	Per Plot Frequency			Total Number	
Species	**Ironwood**	**Control**	**% Down**	**Ironwood**	**Control**
ARBORESCENTS					
Cercidium microphyllum	0.07	0.12	42%	10	17
MEDIUM-SIZED SHRUBS					
Ambrosia dumosa	0.53	1.50	65%	76	215
Atriplex polycarpa	0.22	0.38	42%	31	54
SMALL PERENNIALS					
Spharalcea ambigua	0.28	1.26	78%	40	180
Eriogonum trichopes	0.40	0.72	44%	58	103
Psorothamnus emoryi	0.14	0.22	36%	20	32
MEDIUM-SIZED CACTI					
Opuntia bigelovii	0.04	0.15	73%	6	22

Animal Observations

Our preliminary observations of bird nest frequencies show that even when other trees and large shrubs are present and abundant on a site, ironwood still has a greater than expected influence on bird nesting. On nine 1-ha sites, we found a total of 27 nests in ironwood and only 19 nests in all other species of trees and shrubs combined. Vegetation analysis showed that at these nine sites ironwood was outnumbered by the other trees and shrubs found to contain nests by 18 to 1 (Fig. 12). We also found an increasing use of ironwood by mammals and reptiles as the canopy size increased. Sixty percent of the trees with a canopy average diameter of 9 m or greater have evidence of animal use. Animal use included mammal bedding sites, fecal matter, browsing evidence, packrat nests, and physical observation.

DISCUSSION

The results of this study clearly illustrate the importance of ironwood to the diversity of perennial vegetation in the Gulf Coast subregion of the Sonoran Desert. The dramatic increase in species richness and abundance we observed in perennial vegetation under the canopy of ironwood confirms that this unique desert tree is having a significant impact on the composition of the associated desert flora. Ironwood had its greatest effect on epiphytes, large cacti, vines, large shrubs, small perennials, and medium-sized shrubs, in that order, showing marked increases in both species richness and abundance.

After reviewing prior studies of the close association between large cacti and desert trees (Shreve 1951, McAuliffe 1984), we anticipated that columnar cacti would show a very strong affinity for the canopies of

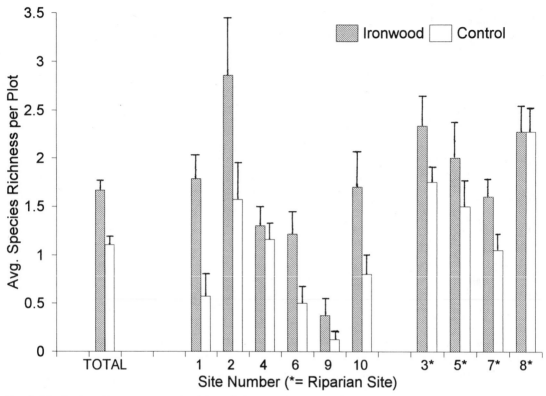

FIG. 7. Distribution of large shrub species richness in ironwood canopy plots and control canopy plots at each site and for the entire study (total includes all 10 sites). Total N=144 and 143 for ironwood and control canopy plots, respectively. Standard error is indicated.

ironwood—as they did. Ironwood is particularly important to the survival of seedlings of these cacti, which are vulnerable to desiccation from high solar radiation, freezing, trampling by cattle and other large herbivores, and perhaps predation. These factors are so important that we observed percentage increases as great as 645% for *Pachycereus pringlei*, 297% for *Lophocereus schottii*, and 173% for *Carnegiea gigantea* under ironwood canopies compared to controls. We frequently observed *L. schottii* growing in rings around the branches of ironwood, suggesting that birds disperse the seeds of this cacti while perching on the tree's outer branches, similar to *C. gigantea* dispersal by doves on *Cercidium microphyllum* (Olin et al. 1989). The 87% increase in large cacti size under ironwood suggests that the favorable conditions under ironwood not only afford protection but also allow cacti to grow more quickly and to greater size than would be possible in more exposed areas. This increased growth would further protect the cacti by allowing them to move more quickly through early growth stages where mortality is presumably high. The influence of ironwood on large cacti may be especially important in maintaining good nest sites and foraging ranges for woodpeckers and pygmy owls, as they depend on the cacti for habitat (Phillips et al. 1964).

In light of ironwood's influence on large cacti, it is interesting to note that we found no changes in the overall species richness or abundance of medium-sized cacti. The vast majority of the medium-sized cacti were *Opuntia*, which are well adapted to exposed conditions. Seedlings of most cacti may benefit greatly from a nurse plant like ironwood, both because of increased soil moisture and protection, but *Opuntia* often avoids the small seedling stage by vegetative propagation. Segments of the *Opuntia* stem will sprout roots when they fall to the ground or are carried away by adhesion to animals. Shreve (1951) noted that *Opuntia* owes some of its abundance to the action of cattle breaking off terminal joints. Although medium-sized cacti showed no increase in diversity under ironwood, there was a substantial rise in average crown size under ironwood when compared to the general habitat (Fig. 11), suggesting that the special conditions under ironwood are favorable for growth but not for establishment or protection (*Opuntia* have little need for protection at any stage in development!).

The effect of ironwood on large shrubs was unquestionably significant. The fact that the more abundant large shrubs, on the whole, show stronger affinities for ironwood than the less abundant large shrubs (Table

3), may support the claim that the abundance of some of these species is directly linked to their ability to utilize the favorable microclimate offered under the canopies of ironwood. It is significant that no large shrub species was found to have an aversion to growing beneath the canopies of ironwood.

Medium-sized shrubs are very common throughout the Sonoran Desert, even on open desert flats (Felger 1966). Extending into exposed habitats, medium-sized shrubs may seem to have little need for the protected microhabitat of ironwood canopies. However, we found medium-sized shrubs to be a heterogeneous growth form with particular species having dramatically varying ecological needs. For example, *Encelia farinosa* and *Simmondsia chinensis* contrast in their niches with *Ambrosia dumosa* and *Atriplex polycarpa*. All are common, widespread, medium-sized shrubs at our study sites, but the first two show dramatic increases in abundance

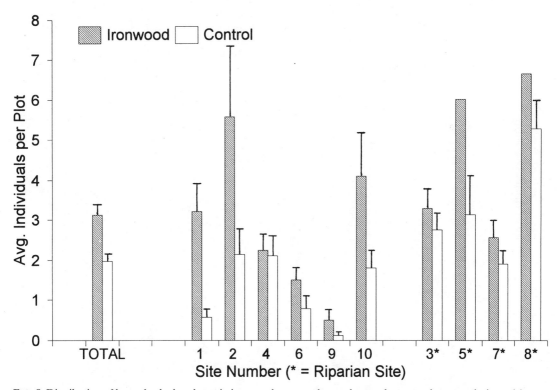

FIG. 8. Distribution of large shrub abundance in ironwood canopy plots and control canopy plots at each site and for the entire study (total includes all 10 sites). Total N=144 and 143 for ironwood and control canopy plots, respectively. Standard error is indicated.

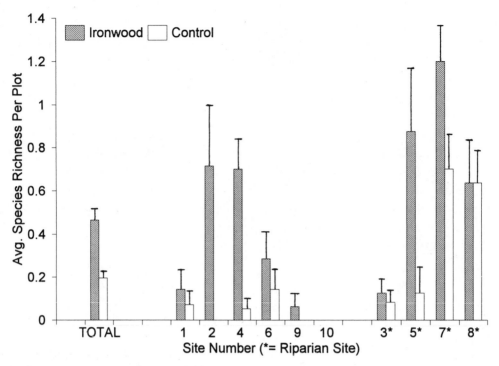

FIG. 9. Distribution of large cacti species richness in ironwood canopy plots and control canopy plots at each site and for the entire study (total includes all 10 sites). Total N=144 and 143 for ironwood and control canopy plots, respectively. Standard error is indicated.

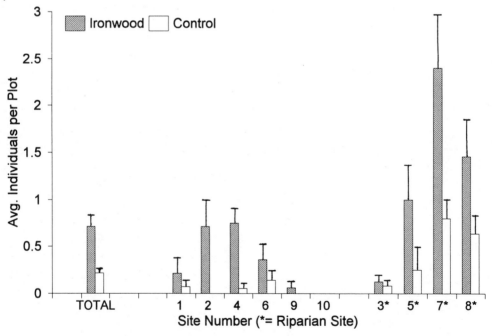

FIG. 10. Distribution of large cacti abundance in ironwood canopy plots and control canopy plots at each site and for the entire study (total includes all 10 sites). Total N=144 and 143 for ironwood and control canopy plots, respectively. Standard error is indicated.

under ironwood canopies, while the second two show dramatic decreases under ironwood (Table 2). Because of counterbalancing differences like this, there is no overall difference in the abundance of medium-sized shrubs as a growth form. Although abundance did not change significantly, there was an increase in the species richness of medium-sized shrubs in the ironwood plots (Fig. 5).

The shaded microenvironment under ironwood provides shrubs with protection from desiccation through decreased evaporation rates and solar radiation, and increased soil moisture and protection at the seedling stage. These factors, combined with the seed bed effect, work to create larger, more diverse shrub populations under ironwood canopies. However, due in large part to increased seedling number and the growth limitations imposed by the overhanging ironwood canopy, the average size of large and medium-sized shrubs under ironwood canopies was slightly smaller than that found in the controls.

Small perennials were the most diverse growth form studied, both under the canopy of ironwood and in control plots (Table 3). Under the ironwood canopy, this growth form exhibited a 63% increase in abundance, a 32% increase in species richness, and a dramatic decrease in N1 diversity index. The increase in abundance can be largely attributed to one species, *Abutilon californicum*, while the increase in species richness is due to an influx of less abundant small perennials that do not appear in the control plots. The increase in average canopy size of small perennials under the ironwood canopy (Fig. 11) may be attributed to a combination of factors including a favorable microhabitat with increased growth rates and the release from any drought-induced growth constraint which might have kept plants small. Additionally, the natural small size of this growth form would allow plants to grow larger without obstruction from the ironwood canopy itself.

From a management perspective, the trends of increased influence of less abundant species in large and medium shrubs and the addition of rare species in small perennials are both very important, because it is these less abundant species that have the highest degree of dependence on the specialized microhabitat under ironwoods. As ironwoods are cut down, these uncommon species will face further restrictions due to their more specific habitat requirements and some populations could conceivably fall below viable levels.

Ironwood did not have an effect on the abundance of trees as a growth form. However, an increased abundance of seedlings under the canopies of ironwood was offset by the decreased number of large trees found there, resulting in the observed average canopy size decrease of trees under ironwoods (Fig. 11). Seedlings gain protection and water, while larger trees are forced to compete with the ironwood for water and sun

TABLE 3. Hill's diversity index for canopy plots and outer ring plots. Hill's N1 Index = e^H (number of abundant species).

Growth Form	Canopy Plots		Outer Ring Plots	
	O. tesota	Control	*O. tesota*	Control
Arborescents	4.431	3.990	4.201	4.228
Large Shrubs	7.208	5.791	4.883	4.830
Medium Shrubs	6.904	6.321	4.641	3.852
Small Perennials	8.232	10.170	9.168	9.400
Annuals	4.384	5.856	6.046	6.551
Large Cacti	2.671	3.196	3.635	3.857
Medium Cacti	3.040	4.136	3.626	3.449
Small Cacti	1.251	1.229	1.000	1.000
Vines	4.774	5.945	2.294	4.293
Epiphytes	1.196	1.000	1.000	1.000

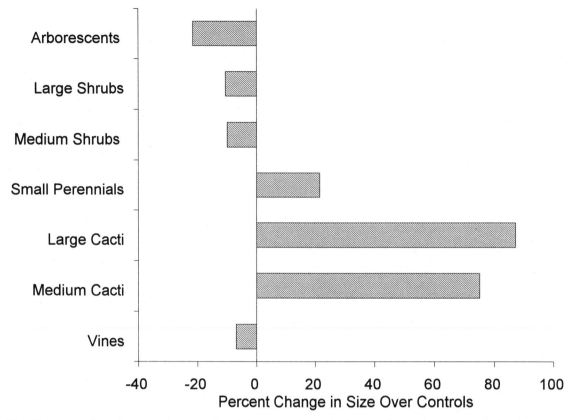

FIG. 11. Percent change in average canopy size of plants growing under ironwood canopies vs. control plots, by growth form.

(McAuliffe 1984). Unlike other trees, not even seedlings of *Cercidium microphyllum* were often found under ironwood. This is noteworthy since these two species often grow together in the same xeroriparian communities. With a 74% decrease in the abundance of *C. microphyllum* under ironwood, competition, or perhaps subtle resource partitioning, may be at work between these two ecologically similar leguminous trees.

As would be expected, large increases were observed in the abundance of vines (250%) and epiphytes (840%) in ironwood canopies. These increases address the critical importance of the structural support ironwood provides for these two growth forms. Because ironwood trees were compared to the general environment and not to other tree species, this study could not speak to the quality of ironwood's structural support of vines and epiphytes in relation to that of other tree species.

The above patterns were determined from the overall results of the study sites when aggregated. However, we found considerable variation in results between the ten different sites we chose (Figs. 2 and 3; and see Appendix I for site descriptions). The most important trend we found when comparing the sites was a substantial dampening of the effect of ironwood at sites with xeroriparian influences when compared to sites without xeroriparian influences (Fig. 4).

Our results support the idea that ironwood provides a microenvironment similar in many respects to a riparian habitat (Fig. 13). At sites without a riparian influence, areas that provide protection, moisture, and shade are very rare, existing almost exclusively under the large trees, most of which are ironwood, thus ironwood plays a large role in increasing the diversity of these areas. The overlap in key habitat qualities is small on these sites, with shade being slightly more available than moisture outside of ironwood canopies, and both these being more available than protection. On riparian influenced sites, shade becomes more widely available outside of the ironwood canopy due to the abundance of deep-rooted riparian tree and shrub species taking advantage of subsurface water. This increased shade creates increased surface soil moisture for plants unable to tap deeper water reserves and the larger structural diversity increases protected habitats for seedling growth.

The relative importance of the different habitat qualities to a given species may in large part determine where it is found: under ironwood, in the more open control plots, or in both areas. A species that requires a relatively large amount of plant-available moisture will be found almost exclusively under ironwood on sites without a riparian influence. As the overall soil moisture increases near a riparian area, this same species may be found growing on control sites and under ironwood

canopies without preference, or, if the species has a secondary preference for sun, it may be found growing almost exclusively in the more open control plots in riparian sites, a complete switch from its habitat of choice at dry sites.

Ironwood was more ecologically important to certain growth forms at some sites than at others, and these differences cannot all be explained by a simple gradient of riparian influence. The factors accounting for these differences may include gradients of latitude, slope, distance from the coast, soil type, tree size, density of stand, cattle grazing, and human impact such as woodcutting. Because our sites were chosen to represent the wide range of habitats in which ironwood is found, it was not possible to isolate any other single factor that correlates directly with the effect of ironwood on diversity and abundance.

This study indicates that indeed there is a higher species richness and abundance of perennial vegetation under the branches of ironwood than in the general

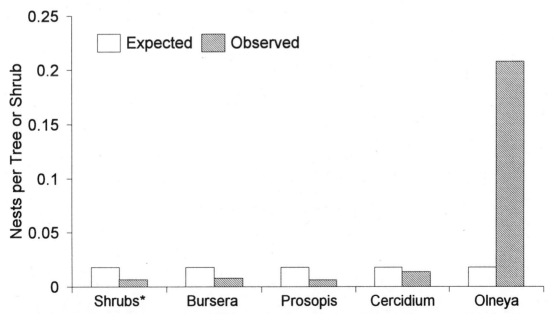

FIG. 12. Observed and expected number of bird nests for nine 1-ha plots. "Nests per tree or shrub" is the number of nests found in a species over the number of individuals of that species found at the sites. N=46 nests. * Shrubs include the seven other species in which nests were found: *Acacia, Colubrina, Condaliopsis, Jatropha, Zizyphus, Viscainoa,* and *Jaquinia.*

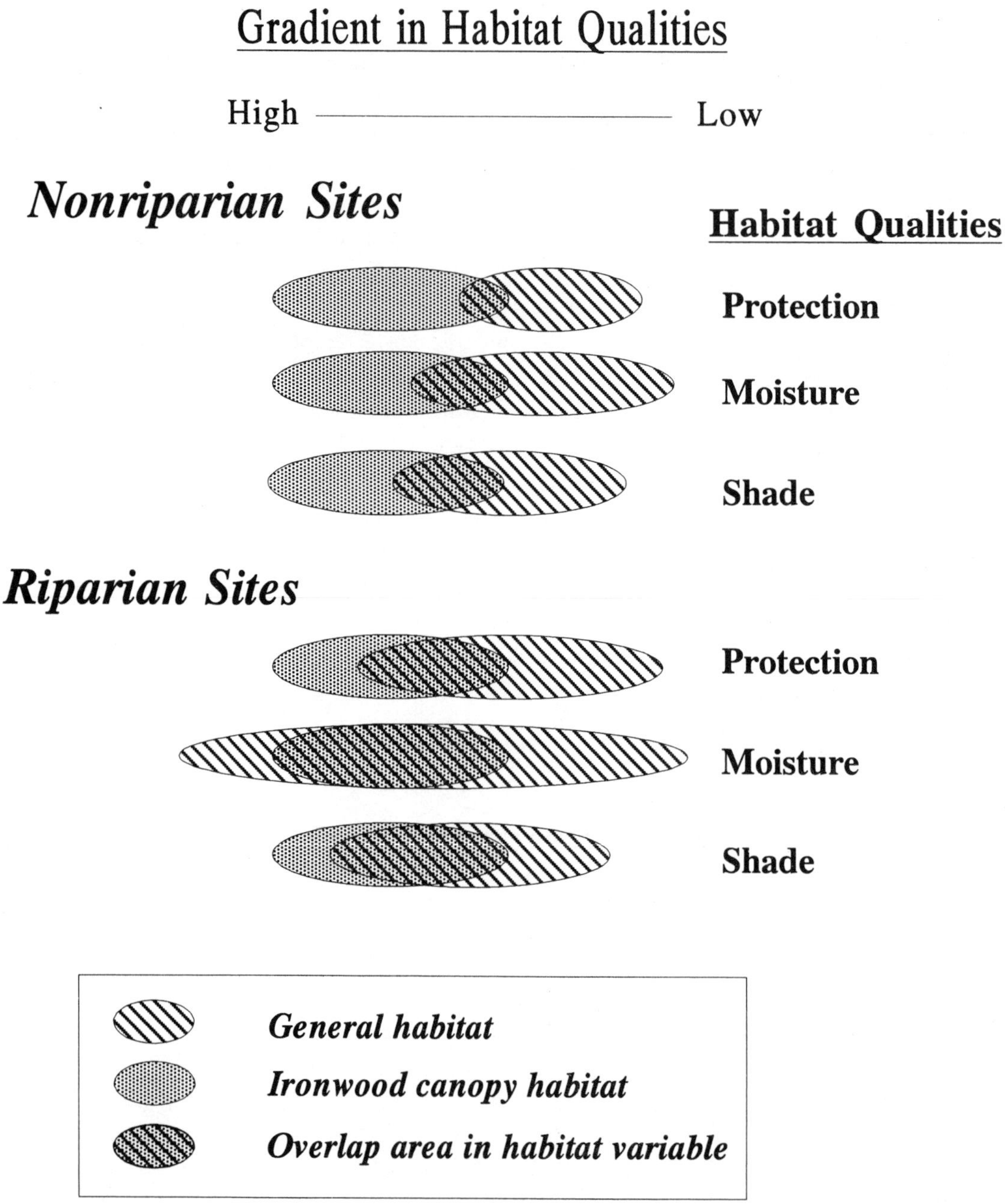

Gradient in Habitat Qualities

High ——————————————— Low

Nonriparian Sites

Habitat Qualities

Protection

Moisture

Shade

Riparian Sites

Protection

Moisture

Shade

General habitat

Ironwood canopy habitat

Overlap area in habitat variable

FIG. 13. Theoretical ranges of three key habitat qualities affecting patterns of perennial plant diversity in the Sonoran Desert and the overlap in these qualities at sites with and without a riparian influence.

habitat. The causes of this increase in diversity lie in the highly integrated, complex web of interactions that has evolved in the Sonoran Desert. Qualities of the micro-habitat under the branches of ironwood that likely contribute to its role as a leading part in the Sonoran Desert include: decreased solar radiation from shade; decreased soil temperatures in summer and increased soil temperatures in winter (Shreve 1931); increased plant-available soil moisture (Shreve 1931, Felger 1966); increased humus (Turner and Brown 1982); nitrogen fixation from rhizobial nodules (Felker and Clark 1981); the seed bed effect; and increased seed dispersal from both perching birds and wind-blown seeds held by the wind-protected canopy.

The factors of shade, soil moisture, soil temperature, and evaporation are intimately connected, and it is this complex of interactions that is likely most important to perennial vegetation. Shreve (1931) observed that shade prolongs the favorable conditions of soil moisture for plants to grow. Shade decreases the temperature of the soil, keeping it cooler than the air, while exposed soils are hotter than the air in summer. Shade decreases evaporation and so maintains a higher plant-available soil moisture for a longer period of time into the dry season. This effectively increases the growing season in the microhabitat under ironwood, and provides extended germination abilities for seeds. Gibson and Nobel (1986) also noted these ameliorating effects of tree shade for cacti species. Patten (1978) found that the combined factors of increased soil moisture and the moderate solar input found under the shade of desert trees appeared to be optimal conditions for ephemeral plants to achieve high rates of photosynthetic efficiency. Although we did not focus on ephemerals in this study, the balance of more soil moisture and decreased water loss due to evapotranspiration may be equally important to the photosynthetic efficiency of perennials as well.

The combination of all the nutrient inputs to the microhabitat under ironwood is what we call the seed bed effect. It begins with the structure of the tree depositing leaves and twigs under its branches and also acting as an anchor for wind-blown organic matter. Because ironwood is a nitrogen-fixing legume (Felker and Clark 1981) nitrogen is added to this bed of humus. Seeds that disperse under the tree encounter the support of an island-like seed bed of rich soil instead of the more sandy or rocky open desert floor. Throughout their life cycles, those plants growing under ironwood further add to the organic matter of the seed bed. In addition, our preliminary observations show that ironwood is used extensively by birds, mammals, reptiles, and ants (e.g., see Fig. 12), which likely bring in more organic matter and disperse seeds under the tree's branches. All told, these factors may change the quality of the soil under ironwood dramatically.

The major factors of increased soil moisture and the seed bed effect under ironwood could be the same for any leguminous desert tree, because their cause is based on the physiognomy of the tree growth form. There are however, many factors that make the quality of the ironwood microhabitat unique among the trees species of the Central Gulf Coast. First, the shade provided by ironwood is more consistently dense than that of other desert trees. Ironwood is the only desert tree that maintains its leaves throughout the dry season. Additionally, ironwood is an unusually slow growing species, living 500-800 years (Ferguson, unpublished; Suzán, pers. comm.). This stability of ironwood as a nurse tree providing a unique microhabitat may be particularly important to the slow-growing columnar cacti. We also observed that the branch structure of ironwood is particularly accommodating to a community of underlying plants, in that branches rarely extend to ground level, and thus there is adequate room for the growth of other plants. Finally, ironwood is unique as a desert tree in its ability to extend into the driest of environments, where the increase in soil moisture found under its branches is most critical to the plant community. Shreve (1951) found ironwood to be most abundant in the drier parts of the Sonoran Desert with less than 200 mm of precipitation. This tree's ability to maintain shade throughout the dry season, to grow big enough to harbor significant growing space under its branches for other species of plants, and to extend its protected microhabitat into the driest of areas makes it uniquely valuable as a desert nurse plant.

Overall, the presence of ironwood causes a marked increase in the stratification of Sonoran Desert communities, creating not only an ecologically more diverse community, but a more structurally diverse community as well. This in turn affects overall faunal diversity (Tomoff 1974, Short 1983), as a more diverse flora affords a larger base for herbivores to feed on and hence more opportunities for primary and secondary predators.

One condition that concerns us is the low rate of ironwood regeneration we found on the Gulf Coast. We observed only five ironwood trees less then 1.5 meters in height on all eight of our mainland sites. Shreve (1951) also found the number of seedlings in all of ironwood's range to be extremely rare. On Tiburón Island, however, we found four young seedlings on only two sites. These preliminary data translate into a ratio of one seedling per 25.8 mature trees on the mainland and one seedling per 6.5 mature trees on the island. This may be partially explained by the fact that there are no cattle on Tiburón. Much grazing has occurred on the mainland, especially in the early 1900's—before Shreve's observation—when there were less controls on overgrazing. Cattle are known to eat the seedlings of many trees, especially during times of drought. However, because ironwood recruitment may be episodic—perhaps occurring 5-10 years per century (Búrquez and Quintana 1994)—these observations remain inconclusive.

CONCLUSIONS

This study illuminates the role of ironwood as a "habitat modifier" species (Mills et al. 1993) in the Sonoran Desert ecosystem. By modifying the habitat under it's branches, ironwood plays a leading part in creating the ecosystem that it occupies, greatly enhancing the diversity of the Sonoran Desert. Yet in many of our sites we noticed cut branches and dead stumps of ironwood. The rate of cutting for carvings and for illegal charcoal production has increased to such an extent that one prominent Seri carver told us that there is only a 2-3 year supply of carvable ironwood left in his local area.

What is the implication of this cutting on the vegetation composition of the Central Gulf Coast subregion of the Sonoran Desert? We would expect a decrease in perennial plant diversity as ironwood cutting continues. Without the seed bed, without the moister shade environment, without the structural support ironwood trees provide, we predict a substantial decline in the more ecologically restricted species that depend on this kind of a microhabitat. Localized extirpations may not follow the loss of ironwood immediately, but without these islands of unique microhabitat, many species will likely decrease in abundance. Decreased population numbers make species, especially uncommon, ecologically restricted ones, more vulnerable to the stochastic perturbations that lead to local extirpations and ultimately to global extinctions.

Ironwood creates a unique microhabitat by its presence, which increases the diversity of the local vegetative community, and though pieces of the microclimate conditions found under ironwood exist elsewhere in the Sonoran Desert—under other tree species, in certain drainages, between certain rock outcroppings—the unique environment that ironwood trees create under their canopies is found no where else. This alone makes the continuing degradation of ironwood untenable.

ACKNOWLEDGMENTS

Our greatest appreciation goes to our good friends Jim Donovin and Kevin Ewing for their enthusiastic participation and skilled ecological research work during the summer of 1992. The four of us were complete partners throughout study design and data collection portions of this project. This project would not have been possible without the generous technical, logistical, and financial support of Gary Nabhan, Tom Fleischner, Humberto Suzán, Richard Felger, Lisa Famolare, Native Seeds/ SEARCH, and Conservation International. We would also like to thank Tom Fleischner and Gary Nabhan for their invaluable criticism of earlier drafts of this document.

LITERATURE CITED

Axelrod, D.I. 1979. Age and origin of the Sonoran Desert vegetation. California Academy of Sciences Occasional Papers 132:1-74.

Búrquez, A. and M. de los Angeles Quintana. 1994. Islands of diversity: Ironwood ecology and the richness of perennials in a Sonoran Desert biological reserve. Pp. 9-27 In: G.P Nabhan and J.L. Carr (eds.), Ironwood: An Ecological and Cultural Keystone of the Sonoran Desert. Conservation International, Occasional Papers in Conservation Biology No. 1.

Davidson, M. 1983. Uncommon Sense: The Life and Thought of Ludwig von Bertalanffy (1901-1972), Father of General Systems Theory. J.P. Tarcher, Los Angeles.

Felger, R.S. 1966. Ecology of the Gulf Coast and islands of Sonora, Mexico. Unpublished dissertation, University of Arizona, Tuscon.

Felger, R.S. and C.H. Lowe. 1976. The island and coastal vegetation and flora of the northern part of the Gulf of California. Contributions in Science. Natural History Museum of Los Angeles County No.285:1-59.

Felker, P. and P.R. Clark. 1981. Nodulation and nitrogen fixation (acetylene reduction) in desert ironwood. Oecologia 48:292-293.

Gibson, A.C. and P.S. Nobel. 1986. The Cactus Primer. Harvard University Press, Cambridge, MA.

Hutto, R.L., J.R. McAuliffe and L. Hogan. 1986. Distributional associates of the saguaro (*Carnegiea gigantea*). Southwestern Naturalist 31:469-476.

King, A.W. 1993. Considerations of scale and hierarchy. Pp. 19-45. *In*: S. Woodley, J. Kay and G. Francis (eds), Ecological Integrity and the Management of Ecosystems. St. Lucie Press, Del Ray Beach, FL.

Ludwig, J.A. and J.F. Reynolds. 1988. Statistical Ecology. Wiley-Interscience Publications. New York.

Mares, M.A., F.A. Enders, J.M. Kingsolver, J.L. Neff., and B.B. Simpson. 1977. *Prosopis* as a niche component of plants and animals. Pp. 123-149. *In:* B. Simpson (ed), Mesquite: Its Biology in Two Desert Ecosytems. Dowden, Hutchinson, and Ross. Stroudsburg, PA.

McAuliffe, J.R. 1984. Saguaro-nurse tree associations in the Sonoran Desert: competitive effects of saguaros. Oecologia 64:319-321.

McAuliffe, J.R. 1990. A rapid survey method for the estimation of density and cover in desert plant communities. Journal of Vegetation Science 1:653-656.

Mills, S.L., M.E. Soulé and D.F Doak. 1993. The keystone-species concept in ecology and conservation. Bioscience 43:219-223.

Olin, G., S.M. Alcorn and J.M. Alcorn. 1989. Dispersal of viable saguaro seeds by white-winged doves (*Zenaida asiatica*). Southwestern Naturalist 34:282-284.

Patten, D.T. 1978. Productivity and production efficiency of an upper Sonoran Desert ephemeral community. American Journal of Botany 65:891-895.

Phillips, A., J. Marshall and G. Monson. 1964. The Birds of Arizona. Univeristy of Arizona Press, Tucson.

Regier, H.A. 1993. The notion of natural and cultural integrity. Pp. 3-18. *In*: S. Woodley, J. Kay and G. Francis (eds), Ecological Integrity and the Management of Ecosystems. St. Lucie Press, Del Ray Beach, FL.

Short, H.L. 1983. Wildlife guilds in Arizona desert habitats. Technical Note 362. U.S. Dept. of the Interior, Bureau of Land Management.

Shreve, F. 1931. Physical conditions in sun and shade. Ecology 12:96-106.

Shreve, F. 1951. Vegetation of the Sonoran Desert. Carnegie Institution of Washington, Publ. 591.

Tomoff, C.S. 1974. Avian species diversity in desert scrub. Ecology 55:396-403.

Turner, R.M. and D.E. Brown. 1982. Sonoran desertscrub. Desert Plants 4:181-187.

Turner, R.M., S.M. Alcorn, G. Olin and J.A. Booth. 1966. The influence of shade, soil, and water on saguaro seedling establishment. Botanical Gazette 127:95-102.

Wiggins, I.L. 1980. Flora of Baja California. Stanford University Press, Stanford, CA.

J.J. Tewksbury
Route 4, Box 114, Brattleboro, VT 05301 USA
C.A. Petrovich
281 South Side Rd., York, ME 03909 USA

APPENDIX I

Site Descriptions

Site #1: Adobe Wash

This coastal bajada site bore a close resemblance to the Torchwood-Cardon series listed by Turner and Brown (1982). The sloping ground was crossed by many reticulate rills (shallow watercourses) embedded in a sandy subsoil covered with larger pebbles and rocks. Opening on the Sea of Cortez and surrounded on three sides by mountainous ridges, the valley received some additional moisture from runoff and occasional coastal fog. Dominant plants included *Bursera microphylla*, *Olneya tesota*, *Colubrina glabra*, *Jatropha cuneata*, *J. cinerea*, *Larrea tridentata* and *Lycium andersonii*. The plot contained 14 ironwood trees, with an average canopy area of 10.56 m^2, the smallest of any site. A fair amount of branch cuts

were observed—including some fresh cuts—and there was minimal evidence of cattle grazing.

Site #2: Tortilla Flat

Tortilla Flat was located on an inland plain facing SW from the rocky hills which it abutted. It was a mixture of reticulate and dendritic watercourses weaving through the shallow slope of the land. The vegetation was similar to the Cacti-Mesquite-Saltbush Series listed by Turner and Brown (1982). Dominant plants included *Prosopis glandulosa* var. *torreyana*, *Lophocereus schottii*, *Pachycereus pringlei*, *Stenocereus thurberi*, *Atriplex polycarpa*, *Apploppaus spinulosus*, *Lycium andersonii* and *Larrea tridentata*. Only seven ironwood trees were found on the site, with an average canopy size of 38.8 m^2, covering 2.7% of the 1-ha site with their canopies. The site was impacted by branch cutting and cattle grazing. Eight cows were seen walking through the site in addition to signs of frequent cattle use.

Site #3: Hummingbird Wash

Located in a riparian wash, Hummingbird Wash was set 6 m below the level of the surrounding creosote flats. There were two main drainages in the river bottom (one 6 m wide by 0.15 m deep; the other 2.5 m wide by 0.16 m deep) with a low terrace, choked with vegetation, between them. The terrace soil was sandy with light gravel, and the sides of the river bottom were rocky and gravelly. The site was more than midway up the mountain slope, and during rainy periods it likely received high moisture input. The vegetation was riparian desertscrub as classified by Felger and Lowe (1976) and dominated by small perennials such as *Abutilon californicum*, *Lyrocarpa coulteri* and *Fagonia californica*. The arborescent vegetation was a mix of small *O. tesota* (avg. canopy area 18.6 m^2), *Bursera microphylla* and *Cercidium microphyllum*. Of the large shrubs, *Larrea tridentata*, *Jatropha cuneata*, *Colubrina glabra* and *Lycium andersonii* were the most common. Some branch cuts and a cattle path just beyond the site were observed.

Site #4: Bee-tongue

Bee-tongue was situated on the high end of a coastal bajada abutting steep mountains on two sides and presented a good example of the Ocotillo-Limberbush-Creosotebush series listed by Turner and Brown (1982). It had two small drains (2 m wide by 0.2 m deep; and 0.7 m wide by 0.4 m deep), and a unique soil type that was gravelly and rocky with protruding limestone bedrock in places. The dominant plants were *Fouquieria splendens*, *Jatropha cuneata* and *Larrea tridentata*, and *Lycium andersonii*. The ironwood was shrubby, with an average height of 3.4 m. Overall the site was low in vegetative cover. No signs of cuts were observed, but there was minimal evidence of cattle.

Site #5: Bosque

Our fifth site was a representation of the mesquite bosque situated in the middle of the Río Magdelana, the major drainage basin of the entire area. Deep dendritic channels (up to 2 m below the level of the vegetation) cut through this site, ranging from 1 m to 10 m in width. These drains were separated by high terraces of very sandy soils, that contained smaller, braided drains. The arborescents were exceptionally large do to the available water. The average canopy size of the eight ironwood trees at this site was 92.9 m², well over twice the size found at any other site. Dominant vegetation included: *Prosopis glandulosa*, *Cercidium microphyllum*, *Lycium andersonii*, *Jatropha cinerea*, *Vallesia glabora*, *Encelia farinosa*, and *Sphaeralcae ambigua*. The cutting and grazing damage at this site was extensive, with cuts up to 1.5 m in diameter, and large cattle paths and bedding areas under the canopies of some ironwoods.

Site #6: Highland

Highland was located on a sloping drainage basin approximately 100 m wide. The wash opened to the southwest and eventually joined the thickly vegetated valley bottom of the Río Magdelana. To the north, the land rose into an upper bajada abutting the crest of coastal mountains. The soil type was mostly sand, although gravelly on the areas between the two wide (3-8 m) and shallow (0.15 m) drains. The vegetation was of the Torchwood-Cardon Series listed by Turner and Brown (1982), with *Cercidium microphyllum* and *Bursera microphylla* dominating the upper canopy along with *Pachycereus pringlei* and large and abundant *Opuntia fulgida*. Large shrubs were much less common than medium shrubs and small perennials. Common medium shrubs included *Lippia palmeri*, *Ambrosa dumosa*, *Encelia farinosa*, and *Simmondsia chinensis*. Small perennials of note included *Eriogonum trichopes*, *Hibiscus dunudotus*, *Horsfordia newberryi*, *Lyrocarpa coulteri* and *Porophyllum gracile*. No cutting was observed, although there was minimal evidence of cattle grazing.

Site #7: Dense *Olneya* Wash

This linear site stretched along a dry streambed which had a very high density of ironwood, with 31 trees. With the average radius of 2.76 m, they covered 7.41% of the site with their canopies. The area was an inland plain or slightly sloping bajada which funneled into the lower Río Magdelana as it cut through the coastal mountains on its way to the Sea of Cortez. The whole site was within 15 m of a 6 m wide, 0.15 m deep channel. The vegetative community was riparian desertscrub, as described by Felger and Lowe (1976). Ironwood was clearly the dominant tree of this xeroriparian community, but also common were *Cercidium microphyllum* and a very large number of *Lophocereus schottii*, with an average of 1.6 individuals encountered per ironwood canopy. All three of the other large cacti were present. Other common species were *Larrea tridentata*, *Ambrosa dumosa*, *A. deltoidea*, *Sphaeralcea ambigua*, *Horsfordia newberryi*, and *Euphorbia xantii*. We found moderate evidence of cutting and cattle grazing.

Site #8: Millipede

Millipede was the most disturbed site in our study, impacted by heavy cutting and grazing, with tire tracks going through some of our plots, many cut branches, and occasional stumps from previous cutting. The site followed the course of a deeply cut, seasonal streambed (up to 1 m deep and never more than 3 m wide). The soils were sandy, with soil lichens growing in sparse patches on the terraces. The vegetation type was riparian desertscrub as classified by Felger and Lowe (1976). The 11 ironwood trees had an average canopy radius of 3.17 m. Aside from these ironwood, the tall vegetation consisted of *Prosopis glandulosa*, *Cercidium floridum*, *C. microphyllum*, as well as *Carnegiea gigantea* and *Lophocereus schottii*. Large shrub growth was the highest of any site, consisting mostly of *Lycium andersonii* and *Larrea tridentata*, with *Jatropha cinerea* and *Acacia greggii* occurring fairly frequently. Also common were *Ambrosa deltoidea*, *A. dumosa*, *Lyrocarpa coulteri*, and *Ambrosia ambrosioides*.

Site #9: Dragonfly Terrace

Located on Isla Tiburón, this site was a terrace of the Río Sauzal river channel. A small drainage crossed the southeast corner of the plot. The soil was very sandy. Vegetation was sparse and low in diversity, due to the absolute dominance of *Encelia farinosa* (5.8 individuals per control plot and 8.5 per ironwood canopy). The 16 ironwood were smaller than average, covering 2.79% of the total site with their canopies. Other arborescents, although uncommon, were *Bursera hindsiana*, *B. microphylla*, and *Cercidium microphyllum*. Large shrubs were almost nonexistent. Common small perennials include *Abutilon californicum*, *Dalea emoryi*, and *Hoffmanseggia intricata*. Cacti were absent except for two *Lophocereus schottii*. No cutting or grazing was found on this island site.

Site #10: Vista San Estebon

Vista San Estebon was a flat mesa dropping slightly, both to the east and west, into larger drainages, and flanked on the north and south by small rocky mountains. Very few drains were found at this site, all of which were reticulate in nature. On the whole, vegetation was sparse, with long interspaces punctuated by large *Prosopis*

glandulosa and the 10 ironwood trees. The ironwood here were larger than in any other site except the Bosque, having an average canopy radius of 3.58 m. Overall vegetational species richness was low, with *Larrea tridentata*, *Encelia farinosa*, *Viscainoa geniculata*, *Abutilon californicum* and *Euphorbia xantii* as common species. Again, no cutting or grazing occurred on this island site.

BOUNDARY EFFECTS ON ENDANGERED CACTI AND THEIR NURSE PLANTS IN AND NEAR A SONORAN DESERT BIOSPHERE RESERVE

Gary Paul Nabhan* and Humberto Suzán

ABSTRACT

Although nominally protected in Organ Pipe Cactus National Monument (a UNESCO Biosphere Reserve), the threatened cactus *Peniocereus striatus* (Brandegee) Buxbaum, continues to be adversely affected by ecological "boundary effects." These effects are due to the contrasting land uses and ecological discontinuities that have developed near the administrative boundary of the reserve. In this case, we test the hypothesis that the cutting of woody legume "nurse plants" for fuel wood, charcoal and tourist crafts indirectly impacts the establishment, growth rate and survivorship of *P. striatus*. Other adverse boundary effects are also identified, and means to reduce their impacts are proposed.

RESÚMEN

Aunque nominalmente protegida en el Parque "Organ Pipe Cactus National Monument" (una reserva de la biosfera de UNESCO), una especie de cactus amenazada *Peniocereus striatus* (Brandegee) Buxbaum, continua siendo afectada ecológicamente en forma negativa por un "efecto de frontera." Este fenómeno se debe al contrastante uso del suelo y discontinuidades ecológicas existentes cerca de las fronteras administrativas de las reservas naturales. En éste caso, probamos la hipótetis de que la corta de leguminosas arbóreas para leña, carbón y artesanías turísticas, afectan indirectamente el establecimiento, las tasas de crecimiento y la sobrevivencia de *P. striatus*. Otros efectos adversos de la frontera son también identificados y se proponen mecanismos para reducir sus impactos.

*To whom correspondence should be addressed.

INTRODUCTION

In efforts to save the rapidly disappearing biological diversity of the Americas, biosphere reserves have become an increasingly popular designation as a conservation strategy (Dasmann 1988; Halffter 1989). This strategy has proven especially attractive in the USA/México border states (Suzán and Fragoso 1989, Reyes-Castillo 1991).

Recently, Mexican conservation officials have proposed the cooperative management of 400,000 ha in a biosphere reserve in México (Sierra el Pinacate, Sonora), with another 400,000 ha UNESCO biosphere reserve on adjacent U.S. lands (Organ Pipe Cactus National Monument "ORPI", and Cabeza Prieta Wildlife Refuge, Arizona). These contiguous protected areas may become the largest nature reserve within any desert biome in the Americas. However, we are reminded that designation and nominal protection of nature reserves is often not enough to insure the continued survival of the rarest species which fall within their boundaries. This is especially true if, a) the boundaries were constructed without cognizance that rare plant or animal populations fall largely on or near the administrative borders of the nature reserve in question, and b) land uses immediately outside the reserve directly or indirectly impact these borderline populations.

In a series of provocative articles, conservation biologist Christine Schonewald-Cox and colleagues have described the boundary effects on parks and reserves. Such effects result in floral and faunal changes once a newly-established administrative boundary has generated a new ecological edge between adjacent and often conflicting land uses (Schonewald-Cox and Bayless 1986). Land uses immediately outside a reserve often generate effects that extend for several hundred meters into the "protected area", such that the generated edge does not necessarily coincide with the administrative boundary of the area. Schonewald-Cox (1988) later gave the example of a desert biosphere reserve (Organ Pipe) as an example where the "natural boundaries" of a particular vegetation type fall just within the administrative boundary of a reserve, leaving much of the biota associated with that vegetation type vulnerable to the prevailing uses beyond the reserve.

What Schonewald-Cox did not know at the time of publication was that at least one of Organ Pipe's rarest plants on the National Park Service sensitive species list occurs only within the generative edge adjacent to the park's administrative boundary with México!

This species is the Sonoran night-blooming cereus, or jaramatraca, *Peniocereus striatus* (Brandegee) Buxbaum, hereafter called the Sonoran cereus cactus. According to the Schonewald-Cox (1988) analysis of the Warren et al. (1981) vegetation map of Organ Pipe, the one plant association within which *P. striatus* occurs is the *Cercidium-Encelia-Stenocereus-Jatropha* association on basalt and rhyolite pediments that make up less than 1% of the total area of the park, and barely enters the United States (Johnson et al. 1990). Within the extension of this habitat into the park is the only legally protected population of this species conserved *in situ*. As one of us has illustrated elsewhere (Nabhan 1992a, b), boundary effects within the areal extent of this habitat falling within the generated edge may be triggering dramatic changes in the demography of this rare species, and of keystone species as well. Suzán et al. (in press) documented the dependency of *P. striatus* regeneration on their sphingid pollinators and on associated woody nurse plants, especially ironwood (*Olneya tesota*) and creosote bush (*Larrea tridentata*). Our objective here is to elucidate the unique and largely unexplored consequences of a rare plant population being located within the generated edge of a nature reserve. In particular, we hypothesize that the rare plant population is significantly affected by the management and uses of the keystone species which happen to direct vegetation processes and/or create microhabitats within the generated edge.

In North American deserts, one special set of keystones are called "nurse plants" (Shreve 1951, Nabhan 1989, Suzán et al. 1989, Valiente-Banuet and Ezcurra

1991); that is, they buffer from environmental stresses a number of less resilient, (usually) understory species that are dispersed and established as seedlings beneath their protective canopies.

In this case, we hypothesize that the legume tree species which are known to serve as nurses for over 160 other species of vascular plants (see Plant Names List), are particularly important to rare succulents at the extremes of their distribution ranges (Table 1). The two species that we believe function as microhabitat forming keystones at ORPI for *P. striatus* are *Olneya tesota* Gray, hereafter called ironwood, and *Prosopis velutina* (Woot.) Woot. & Standley, one of the three mesquite species in the area, hereafter called velvet mesquite. These same nurses also serve a number of other rare or endemic cacti of the area: *Peniocereus greggii, Echinomastus erectocentrus* var. *acunensis, Lophocereus schottii, Mamillaria thornberi,* and *Stenocereus thurberi,* all considered "sensitive plants" of Organ Pipe Cactus National Monument by U.S. National Park Service biologists.

To test the hypotheses mentioned above, we will first characterize the vegetation type found along the administrative boundary and cite which ecological conditions developing within this landscape demonstrate that it is currently forming a generated edge. Second, we will describe the Sonoran cereus cactus in relation to its location and association with (hypothesized) keystone legumes. Third, we will document depletion of the ironwood and velvet mesquite cover within the generated edge of the reserve. Fourth, we will evaluate the effects of keystone removal on cereus cacti.

MATERIALS AND METHODS

Study Site

Organ Pipe Cactus National Monument (ORPI), located in western Pima County, Arizona, USA, lies adjacent to the Municipio de Plutarco Elias Calles, Sonora, México (Fig. 1).

Using the vegetation map produced by Warren et al. (1981) on contract for the National Park Service, we identified the plant association where the Sonoran cereus cactus was known to occur from earlier studies (Johnson et al. 1990). Because the vegetation map does not cover areas across the USA/México border, we used indicator species, soils, and topography identified by Warren et al. (1981) to guide us in sampling adjacent Mexican lands, then sampled the entire vegetation community once the Sonoran cereus cactus was found. Using this stratified sampling technique, we documented perennial species composition, and estimated the abundance and percent ground cover according to the logarithmic plot method (McAuliffe 1990), with 250 m^2 circular plots for our upland samples, and rectangular plots centered on watercourse midlines for our wash samples. The ephemeral watercourses, or "washes", that we sampled are described below.

Cereus Cactus Autoecology

Over more than 200 hours of ground surveying, we encountered a minimum of 115 individual plants of Sonoran cereus cactus within the 1000 m on either side

TABLE 1. Rare plants detected beneath the canopy of ironwood.

Scientific Name	Family	Common Name
Fouquieria columnaris	Fouquieriaceae	cirio
Echinomastus erectocentrus var. *acunensis*	Cactaceae	acuña
Mamillaria thornberi	Cactaceae	biznaguita
Peniocereus greggii	Cactaceae	jaramatraca
Peniocereus striatus	Cactaceae	jaramatraca
Tumamoca macdougallii	Cucurbitaceae	camote de jabali

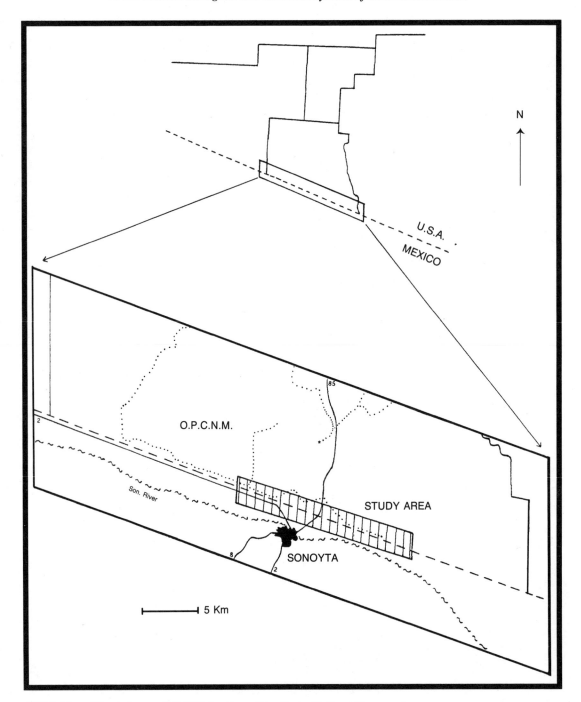

FIG. 1. Map of the study area. O.P.C.N.M. = Organ Pipe Cactus National Monument.

of the international boundary. Elsewhere in Organ Pipe, Johnson et al. (1990) and other endangered plant surveys have failed to encounter other populations after many man-months of sampling. Felger (1992) failed to encounter other populations of cereus cactus in northwest Sonora after 20 years of plant collecting.

For each individual found, we recorded the presence or absence, identity, and distance from the main stem of the nearest perennial potentially shading the main shoot of the Sonoran cereus cactus. We also used frequency data derived from the above vegetation sampling to compare with frequency data of nurse plants associated with Sonoran cereus cactus, analyzing these by a chi square test (Zar 1984). Finally, within the 500 m^2 around the 250 m^2 sample plots, we made random tosses of metal rings and measured distances from perennial nurses to compare with the distances from the Sonoran desert cacti to their nurses, comparing these distances via the t-test (Zar 1984).

The allometric characteristics of the Sonoran cereus plants, and a more detailed discussion of the nurse plant-cacti relationships were described in Suzán et al. (in press).

Ironwood and Mesquite Depletion

On 14 ephemeral watercourses crossing the border in the area, all 5 m or more wide, we established strip sample plots (10 x 100 m) from the road adjacent to the international border and at 100 m within each country. We used these plots to estimate the number of trees 2 m tall (or taller), in particular mesquites, ironwoods and other woody legumes; the number of trees with one or more branches sawed or ax-cut by humans; the number of dead trunks identifiable as legumes; and evidence of natural mortality. The 14 watercourses cross the border in a range of 12 km, and span the range of all Sonoran cereus cactus known on the park boundary.

The status of the fourteen watercourses is as follows. Two watercourses among the fourteen washes coalesce in the USA within 200 m, and five more were obliterated south of the border by agriculture; two at 100 m south of the border, and one more coalesces 150 m within México. This leaves 14 strip transects for the first 100 m and 13 for 100-200 m in USA, 10 for the first 100 m and seven for the 100-200 m in México.

In addition, we sampled five of the watercourses 500 m within the USA, and eight (100x10 m) strip transects in upland sites for each country on volcanic slopes 2-15 m above the silty and sandy water courses.

These upland sites occur in each country within the first 500 m from the border, within the range of the Sonoran cereus cactus subpopulations.

The names and sampling intensity of each strata were: USA100 (100-200m within USA) 14 transects; USA200 (200-300m within USA) 13 transects; USA500 (500-600m within USA) five transects; USAupl (USA uplands) eight transects; MEX100 (100-200m within México) 10 transects; MEX200 (200-300m within México) seven transects; and MEXupl (México uplands) eight transects.

The percentages of legume damaged and of legume deaths for each group were compared by a one-way analysis-of-variance, after an arcsine transformation of the percentages. Finally, we prepared contingency tables to evaluate the relative "health status" of each Sonoran cereus cactus associated with cut or uncut nurses. The conditional evaluation categories were severely damaged, moderately damaged, minor damage, or no damage; evaluated by the same investigator (H.S.) during the same winter (1993).

RESULTS

Cereus Cactus Autoecology

The Sonoran cereus cactus population at the border site of Sonoyta-Organ Pipe was distributed in four small discrete subpopulations, each on a small volcanic mountain with pediment soils, and with ephemeral watercourses running beneath these rocky hills. Two of the subpopulations were located in the USA (USA1 and USA2), and two in México (MEX1 and MEX2). The degree of disturbance was strongest at MEX2, a site located close to a garbage dump.

The total area occupied by the population, including the intermediate uplands and watercourses, was approximately 60 ha, located within a 1.5 km x 2 km area along the border. The specific density for each subpopulation, and the subpopulation sizes are presented in Fig. 2. Because the plants exhibited a "vine-like" (scandent) growth form, obtaining support from the closest shrubs

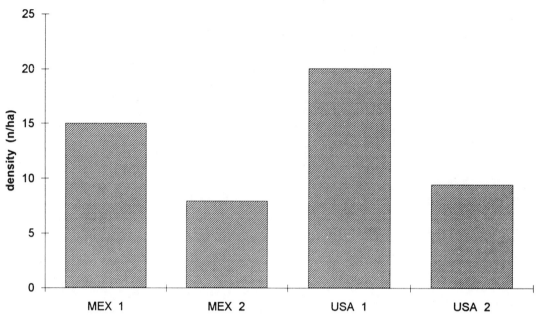

FIG. 2. Number of individuals and density for the four discrete subpopulations of *P. striatus*. For Mex1, Mex2, and USA1, n=35 in each case; for USA2, n=10.

and trees, the branches were easily broken. However, the cactus stems easily regenerated through basal resprouting. Therefore, our attempts to represent the size classes of the population proved useless (Suzán et al., in press).

The distances from the Sonoran cereus cactus plants to the closest perennial were significantly shorter than those of the random points to the closest perennial (Pr t=[2.22/131.2 df]=0.03), indicating a strong positive association of these cereus with their nurses.

Ironwood is the tree most frequently associated with Sonoran cereus cactus, serving as its principal nurse at this locality. We recorded 30.9% of the cereus growing beneath its canopies, but ironwood contributed only 6.2% of the total canopy area in our sample plots (Fig. 3). Ironwood and the other two major legumes (mesquite and little leaf palo verde) provided more than 50% of the nurse plants used by these cacti, but contributed only 35% of the perennial cover in the community. Thus, these legumes importance to the cacti was disproportionate to the relative dominance in the community.

TABLE 2. Legume densities and number of damaged and dead trees in the different sampling groups in the Organ Pipe-Sonoyta border region.

Site	trees/1000m^2		damaged trees/1000 m^2		dead trees/1000 m^2		N
	Mean	S.Error	Mean	S.Error	Mean	S.Error	
USA100	37.28	3.52	11.78	1.59	3.14	1.25	14
USA200	34.61	3.90	9.46	1.72	1.92	0.54	13
MEX100	32.20	8.66	8.80	2.05	1.90	0.86	10
MEX200	32.42	6.39	10.28	2.51	4.86	1.24	7
USA500	21.60	6.72	2.60	0.87	0.60	0.40	5
USAupl	17.75	4.63	1.62	0.53	0.25	0.16	8
MEXupl	8.37	1.21	4.50	0.42	0.50	0.18	8

Mesquite and Ironwood Depletion

Severe habitat disturbances on the Mexican sites were detected during the study. Three of the fourteen washes were obliterated by the expansion of urban settlements within the Sonoyta municipality, and two others were disrupted by agricultural fields south of the border.

Legume density and the number of dead and damaged trees were higher in the washes (USA100, USA200, MEX100, MEX200, USA500) than on the hills and upland slopes (Table 2). In general, the relative proportion of trees damaged was greatest for the MEXupl transects. The legume species reported in the transects were mesquite (*P. velutina*), ironwood (*O. tesota*), blue palo verde (*Cercidium floridum*), little leaf palo verde (*C. microphyllum*), catclaw acacia (*Acacia greggii*) and whitethorn acacia (*Acacia constricta*).

An inverse relationship between the densities of ironwood and mesquite was detected, where mesquite decreased in number from the watercourses to the uplands (Table 3). Ironwood, relatively scarce in washes,

became more evident in the uplands. Ironwood also increased in the watercourses as we moved northward and up slope (Table 4).

A similar trend was detected for the number of ironwood and mesquite left dead and damaged, being higher for mesquites in the watercourses, and higher for ironwood in the uplands (Tables 3 and 4). The highest levels of dead and damaged ironwoods were on the Mexican uplands, where 70 individuals of Sonoran cereus cactus were located, comprising 60% of the total population.

Significant differences were detected between the higher percentages of damaged trees in the Mexican uplands compared with all the ORPI sites. All Mexican sites exhibited relatively higher levels of disturbance, and the site with the smallest percentage of damaged trees was that of the USA500 (Fig. 4). There were non-statistically significant differences regarding the number of dead trees, but also the Mexican sites experienced higher percentages of dead trees than in the U.S. sites (Fig. 5). The effects of harvesting activities were ob-

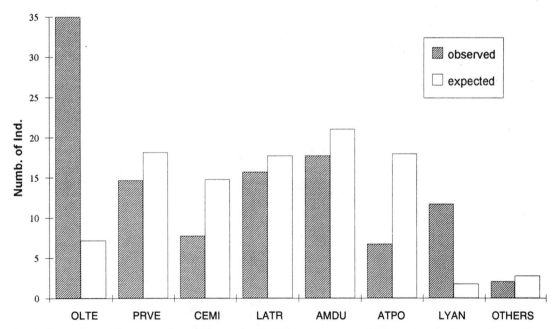

FIG. 3. Comparison of the observed nurse frequencies (n=113) and the expected frequencies according to the contribution of each species to the community. $P(\chi^2=173.74, 7 \text{ df})<0.001$. OLTE=*Olneya tesota*; PRVE=*Prosopis velutina*; CEMI=*Cercidium microphyllum*; LATR=*Larrea tridentata*; AMDU=*Ambrosia dumosa*; ATPO=*Atriplex polycarpa*; LYAN=*Lycium andersonii*.

TABLE 3. Mesquite densities and number of damaged and dead trees in the different sampling groups in the Organ Pipe-Sonoyta border region.

Site	trees/1000m^2		damaged trees/1000 m^2		dead trees/1000 m^2		N
	Mean	S.Error	Mean	S.Error	Mean	S.Error	
USA100	25.00	3.23	10.35	1.56	3.00	1.26	14
USA200	22.38	3.35	8.07	1.51	1.92	0.54	13
MEX100	16.30	3.19	7.00	2.08	1.80	0.85	10
MEX200	17.28	4.77	8.14	2.34	3.85	0.99	7
USA500	6.40	2.42	1.40	0.74	0.40	0.40	5
USAupl	1.25	0.36	0.12	0.12	0.00	0.00	8
MEXupl	1.37	0.53	0.75	0.25	0.00	0.00	8

TABLE 4. Ironwood densities and number of damaged and dead trees in the different sampling groups in the Organ Pipe-Sonoyta border region.

Site	trees/1000m^2		damaged trees/1000 m^2		dead trees/1000 m^2		N
	Mean	S.Error	Mean	S.Error	Mean	S.Error	
USA100	3.14	0.99	0.78	0.33	0.07	0.07	14
USA200	3.93	1.68	0.84	0.37	0.08	0.07	13
MEX100	1.50	0.61	0.40	0.22	0.10	0.10	10
MEX200	1.42	0.68	0.57	0.43	0.43	0.29	7
USA500	6.20	2.61	1.20	0.58	0.20	0.20	5
USAupl	9.37	2.15	1.12	0.44	0.25	0.16	8
MEXupl	4.50	0.72	2.75	0.49	0.50	0.18	8

served for a distance of at least 500 m beyond the USA border into the biosphere reserve, suggesting to us that the "generated edge" may be 0.5 to 1 km wide. However, the damage within the U.S. was restricted to the removal of branches, presumably for use as kindling by Mexican neighbors. The exception to this trend in the USA was in a wash close to a historic ranching settlement, where the number of damaged and dead trees was unusually high. This damage may have begun during the ranching era prior to the establishment of the park in 1937, but may be continued by Mexican residents living within a few hundred meters of the ranch house on the other side of the border.

The relative "apparent health" of each Sonoran cereus cactus and the amount of damage detected on each nurse plant were significantly correlated using Kendall's Tau C, and these two variables seem to be positively associated (Fig. 6). No mortality of cereus plants was detected beneath healthy nurses with undam-

aged canopies. The plants on the Mexican side of the border were in poorer condition due to the damage and removal of nurse plants by wood cutters. (All eight nurses recently removed from their sites were in the Mexican subpopulations.)

DISCUSSION

The México-USA border in the Organ Pipe-Sonoyta area represents a clear case of habitat fragmentation as a result of contrasting land uses, and the imposition of artificial boundaries onto natural communities. Fragmentation of habitats has been recognized as one of the major threats to biological diversity (Harris 1984), dramatically affecting the survival of rare and endangered species (Soulé and Kohn 1989). All four subpopulations of Sonoran cereus cactus in the study area have suffered from the differential ecological impacts resulting from divergent land uses, and these impacts are especially

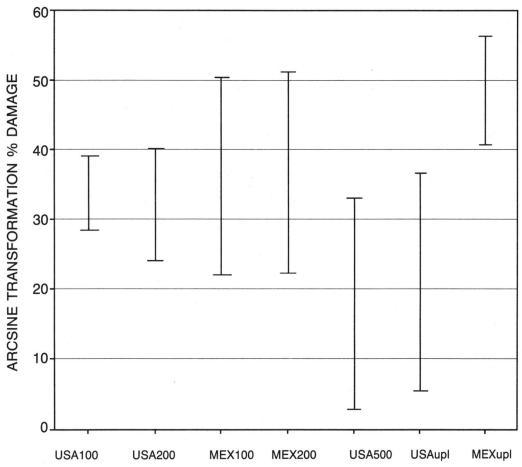

FIG. 4. A comparison of the arcsine transformation for the damaged trees percentage with ANOVA 95% confidence intervals (Duncan). ANOVA Pr=(f=3.63/6, 58 df)=0.004.

evident in México.

The population of Sonoran cereus cactus in the study area exhibited a strong association with the nurse plants, being particularly dependent on the thorny canopies of legumes for protection. The long-lived ironwood was especially important. This result reinforces those reported by Suzán et al. (in press) where non-significant differences were found among the distances from cacti to nurse plants for the four subpopulations (USA1, USA2, MEX1, MEX2), and the cacti tended to be situated in the southern shade provided by the nurses. Sensitive cacti beneath nurses gained more protection against frosts in winter, a strong limiting factor on the survival of cactus populations near the northern edges of

their range (Nobel 1980).

The major threats to Sonoran cereus cactus in the region were the habitat fragmentation due to urban growth and agricultural activities within Sonoyta, and the woodcutting of nurse legumes, both in watercourses and in upland habitats. Suzán et al. (in press) also reported the spraying of pesticides and its effect on the sphingid moth pollinators as an important local threat to the reproduction of Sonoran cereus cacti near agricultural areas. However, our efforts have halted the U.S. subsidized pesticide spraying in Sonora adjacent to the park.

The accelerated rate of tree legume depletion in the Mexican state of Sonora for charcoal and carvings

(Mellink et al. 1991, Nabhan 1992b) has reached the Sonoyta region, as indicated by the percentages of damaged and dead trees in the Mexican transects. Park law enforcement officers have recently apprehended Mexican woodcutters hauling one metric ton of ironwood out of the park through a cut in the border fence.

The deforestation in the Sonoyta region is the result of woodcutting for charcoal production, brick foundries, tourist crafts, and vegetation conversion to exotic pasture grasses, the latter land use change having occurred on more than 193,000 hectares in Sonora since 1965.

The higher levels of impact observed in Mexican uplands and bajadas can be explained by the fact that ironwood trees in this area were exploited by craftsmen for the excellent quality of its dry wood, which is favored over that extracted from more mesic watercourses. In contrast, the extraction and damage of mesquites, ironwood and other legumes in Mexican watercourses can be best explained by the growing demand for charcoal production and local fuelwood consumption.

In the USA, high levels of damage have not penetrated too far beyond the border (1 km), but borderside woodcutting has clearly affected the distributional range of the Sonoran cereus cactus in Organ Pipe, because, unfortunately, all known individuals of this cactus grow within 500 m of the border. The bulk of the woodcutting in the biosphere reserve has been done

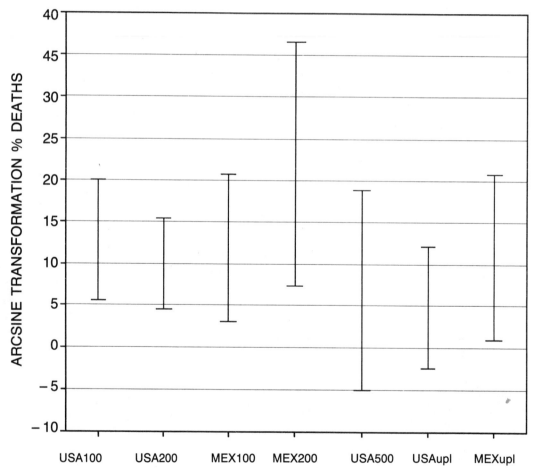

FIG. 5. A comparison of the arcsine transformation for the dead trees percentage with ANOVA 95% confidence intervals (Duncan). No statistical differences between means were detected. ANOVA Pr=(f=1.625/6, 58 df)=0.156.

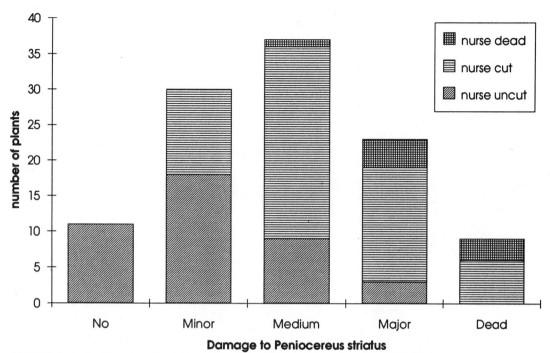

FIG. 6. Relative health status of each *P. striatus* and its associated nurse plant. (N=110). χ^2 independence test= P(χ^2= 50.67/8 df)<.00001. Kendall's Tau C=P(K=0.5286)<.00001.

clandestinely by the unemployed farm working families living just across the border who are unable to pay the higher prices for wood or charcoal that restaurants and tourists pay in Sonoyta. Wood prices have quadrupled in Sonoyta over the last decade, reaching $300 U.S. per cord by 1991. Historically, both ranchers and campers were responsible for removing quantities of live and dead wood from the Organ Pipe area.

The connection between damaged nurses and the "deteriorating health" of the cereus cacti could lead to the local extirpation of the species in the study area. If the Mexican subpopulations are progressively eliminated, the USA subpopulation could not long sustain viable population levels with only 45 individuals, not all of which are reproductive. Considering the minimum numbers required to avoid genetic drift and inbreeding depression (Simberloff 1988), this obligately outcrossing species may already be approaching such minima for the region. We have already detected low seed set and premature loss of developing fruit during three years of observation.

The possible solutions to this problem must include a reorientation of "users" in both countries. On one hand, the National Park Service staff must begin to more positively interact with their Mexican neighbors, implementing the biosphere reserve buffer zone concept, where the benefits of the reserve can be tangibly extended to its neighbors. Organ Pipe's interpretive staff is planning educational outreach to Mexican neighbors to begin in 1994. This environmental education program planned by Mexican and American educators will hopefully be a means to reinforce conservation messages appropriate for the communities surrounding the biosphere reserve.

Only when the uninhabited areas of the biosphere reserve are considered more than an easily-accessible source of fuelwood will further destruction be averted. At the same time, American visitors to the reserve and its adjacent Mexican border town must accept responsibility for the effects of their consumerism, because the purchase of tourist crafts and cheap barbecued meals has aggravated the local fuelwood shortage, driving those with the least resources to the other side of the border in search of fuelwood. Ultimately, American consumerism and the resulting inequalities apparent along the border must also be addressed.

ACKNOWLEDGMENTS

This project was funded by USFWS-SEDUE border projects, the naturalist John Hay, Center for Environmental Studies (ASU) and Pew Scholars Program in Conservation and Environment. We thank Jim Barnett, Caroline Wilson and other rangers from Organ Pipe Cactus National Monument for innumerable courtesies.

LITERATURE CITED

Dasmann, F.R. 1988. Biosphere reserves, buffers and boundaries. Bioscience 38:487-489.

Felger, R. 1992. Synopsis of the vascular plants of northwestern Sonora, México. Ecológica 2(2):11-44.

Halffter, G. 1989. Reflexiones sobre las reservas de la biosfera en México. BIOTAM 1(1):6-8.

Harris, L.D. 1984. The Fragmented Forest. Univ. Chicago Press, Chicago.

Johnson, R.A., M.A. Baker, D.J. Pinkava, N. Trushell,and G.A. Ruffner. 1990. Special status plants of Organ Pipe Cactus National Monument, Arizona, Sensitive Ecosystems Project, Final Report. Ruffner Associates, Prescott, AZ.

McAuliffe, J.R. 1990. A rapid survey method for the estimation of density and cover in desert plant communities. Journal of Vegetation Science 1:653-656.

Mellink, E., G. Nabhan, and H. Suzán. 1991. Ironwoodtree/ El palo fierro (*Olneya tesota*). CEDO News 4(2):27-30.

Nabhan, G.P. 1989. Nurse plant ecology of threatened desert plants. Pp. 377-383. *In*: T. Elias (ed), Conservation and Management of Rare and Endangered Plants. Proceedings of a Confer-ence of the California Native Plant Society.

Nabhan, G.P. 1992a. Cryptic cacti on the borderline. Pp. 108-115. *In:* T.J. Lyon and P. Stine (eds), On Nature's Terms. Texas A&M Univ. Press, College Station.

Nabhan, G.P. 1992b. Desert rescuers. World Monitor 7(5):36-41.

Nobel, P.S. 1980. Morphology, surface temperatures, and northern limits of columnar cacti in the Sonoran Desert. Ecology 61:1-7.

Reyes Castillo, P. 1991. Las reservas de la biosfera en México: Ensayo histórico sobre su protección. BIOTAM 3(1):1-8.

Schonewald-Cox, C.M. 1988. Boundaries in the protection of nature reserves. BioScience 38:480-486.

Schonewald-Cox, C.M. and J.W. Bayless. 1986. The boundary model: a geographical analysis of design and conservation of nature reserves. Biological Conservation 38:305-322.

Shreve, F. 1951. Vegetation of the Sonoran Desert. Carnegie Institution of Washington, Publ. 591.

Simberloff, D. 1988. The contribution of population and community biology to conservation science. Annual Review of Ecology and Systematics 19:473-511.

Soulé, M.E. and K.A. Kohm. 1989. Research Prioritiesfor Conservation Biology. Island Press, Washington, DC.

Suzán, H. and C. Fragoso. 1989. Investigación y conservación en la reserva de la biosfera el Cielo. BIOTAM 1(3):48-53.

Suzán, H., G. Malda, J. Jiménez, L. Hernández, M. Martínez, and G.P. Nabhan. 1989. Evaluación de plantas amenazadas y en peligro de extinción en el estado de Tamaulipas. BIOTAM 1(1):20-27.

Suzán, H., G.P. Nabhan, and D. Patten. In Press. Nurse plant and floral biology of a rare night-blooming cereus, *Peniocereus striatus* (Brandegee) Buxbaum. Conservation Biology.

Valiente-Banuet, A. and E. Ezcurra. 1991. Shade as a cause of the association between the cactus *Neobuxbaumia tetetzo* and the nurse plant *Mimosa luisiana* in the Tehuacán Valley, México. Journal of Ecology 79:961-972.

Warren, P.L., B.K. Morteson, B.D. Ttreadwell, J.E. Bowers, and K.L. Reichardt. 1981. Vegetation of Organ Pipe Cactus National Monument. Technical Report No. 8. Cooperative National Park Resources Study Unit. University of Arizona, Tucson.

Zar, J.H. 1984. Biostatistical Analysis. Prentice-Hall. N.J.

G.P. Nabhan
Conservation International and
Arizona-Sonora Desert Museum
2021 North Kinney Road
Tucson, AZ 85743 USA
H. Suzán
Center for Environmental Studies
Arizona State University
Tempe, AZ 85281 USA

IRONWOOD AND ART: LESSONS IN CULTURAL ECOLOGY

Sara St. Antoine

ABSTRACT

A growing number of conservation organizations support nature-based handicraft markets in threatened habitats as a way to sustain both local resources and local culture. Despite the obvious strengths of such initiatives, their potential pitfalls have not yet been sufficiently described. This report provides a broad critical review of the artisan program accompanying desert ironwood tree conservation in Sonora, México. The Ironwood Alliance—a binational, mulitcultural team of scientists and crafts-promoters directing the ironwood conservation strategy—began working with Seri and Mexican woodcarvers in 1991. The alliance has introduced or encouraged a wide variety of alternative materials to reduce demand on ironwood. They have organized exhibits and produced brochures to increase buyer education about Sonoran artisans. Finally, they have worked to ensure proper labelling and certification of ironwood products. Each decision has generated its own dilemmas; among them, the danger of interfering with local politics, artistic integrity, and community structure. Concerns about the sustainability of any kind of ironwood harvesting remain. It is hoped that the problem solving strategies and solutions particular to the ironwood program may provide insights into other artisan projects worldwide.

RESÚMEN

Un número creciente de organizaciones conservacionistas apoyan la apertura de mercados para la artesanía de productos de uso sostenible provenientes de los hábitats amenazados, con el fín de proteger los recursos naturales y la cultura local. A pesar de las buenas intenciones de tales iniciativas, su peligro potencial no ha sido suficientemente analizado. Este informe proporciona una revisión crítica ámplia de un programa de artesanías que es parte de un proyecto de conservación de los árboles de palo fierro en Sonora, México. La Alianza Pro Palo Fierro—un equipo binacional y multicultural de científicos y promotores de artesanos que dirigen la estratégia para la conservación del palo fierro—empezó a trabajar con talladores Seri y Mexicanos en 1991. En los años siguientes, la Alianza ha presentado y estimulado el uso de una gran variedad de materiales alternativos al palo fierro para reducir la demanda. Este grupo ha organizado exhibiciones y producido folletos de información para aumentar la educación de los compradores sobre la artesanía de Sonora. Finalmente, ha trabajado en asegurar el reconocimiento y certificación de los productos de palo fierro. Sin embargo, cada decisión ha generado dilemas, entre ellos; el peligro de interferir con las políticas locales, integridad artística, y la estructura de la comunidad. Además, todavía existen dudas sobre la sostenibilidad de cualquier tipo del uso de palo fierro. Sin embargo, se espera que los resultados proporcionados por el programa del palo fierro puedan aportar perspectivas para otros programas a nivel mundial.

INTRODUCTION

In the clamor to slow this planet's rapid decline in species, another kind of extinction has often been missed: the loss of indigenous languages, traditional arts, and knowledge of the ways local resources can be used to heal, feed, shelter, decorate. Biological and cultural declines are not simply parallel; they are often interlinked. With this in mind, a growing number of conservation organizations have developed programs designed to sustain a community's cultural heritage as well as its natural resource base. One popular strategy has been to market traditional handicrafts created from local materials, such as wood, vines, natural dyes, and stones. With tourism and international import markets at all-time highs, handicrafts—especially those made in developing nations—carry the economic potential that conservationists dream about. The reality of these endeavors, however, is often one of tremendous challenges and potentially damaging impacts to the very cultures and resources they are designed to protect.

The conservation strategy for ironwood (*Olneya tesota*) provides a telling example with which to examine these impacts. Ironwood is considered not only a keystone species in its desert habitat, but also a cornerstone to the crafts-based economies of Seri Indian and Mexican communities of Sonora, México. For this reason, the Ironwood Alliance has made artisan development a central component of its conservation strategy. Both progress and setbacks have marked the Alliance's path, and every step has been weighted with unexpected dilemmas. While no simple recipe for success, the ironwood story elucidates important themes likely to pertain to any handicraft initiative.

The first part of this paper describes the primary cultural, social, and ecological concerns handicrafts markets elicit. The second part examines the case of iron-wood carving in the context of these broader issues, outlining and evaluating the efforts to date of the Iron-wood Alliance.

HANDICRAFTS AND CONSERVATION—A GLOBAL PERSPECTIVE

Outside intervention in the area of craft production can cause irreplaceable damage to indigenous ways of life, deteriorating social organization and affecting self-image and ethnic identity. In other words, we must check to see at which point craft production for the market can alter the principle social institutions which bring order to indigenous life, as well as the ecosystem of which the native is part.
B.Ribiero in Israel and Guerre (1982)

While handicrafts production may sound like an obscure industry unlikely to have significant economic potential, such is not the case. The sale of handicrafts now constitutes the second largest source of income in developing countries, trailing only agriculture (Popelka and Littrell 1991). With the rise in international tourism, coupled with increased consumer interest in exported goods, the market for these items has expanded both within the country of origin and in other countries. Given this success, handicraft production is being widely touted as an important economic development strategy. In Latin America, it is among the forms of household production said to be crucial amidst the current debt crisis (Nash 1991).

Economic benefits are not the only reason handicrafts have been promoted. In many cases, they tie into broader efforts of cultural preservation. Viewed by outsiders as "traditional art," these crafts are often objects that have historically served specific utilitarian or religious functions within a community. They became obsolete when modern alternatives were introduced, or when new customs and religions barred or precluded their use. Common replacements for traditional wares include plastic buckets for earthenware jars, metal utensils for wooden ones, or nylon bags for handwoven baskets.

With this transition from handmade to traded or storebought goods, the incentive to perpetuate handicrafts was diminished. In many places, crafts died out once children of artisans came to view them as unprofitable enterprises (Graburn 1976). And, because traditional crafts often make use of native resources, their loss has often been accompanied by the disappearance within a single generation of information about the identity of local resources, and their uses (Milton 1992).

Against this backdrop of change, markets for handicrafts offer an incentive to retain traditional knowledge and skills, and may also strengthen ethnic identity and cultural pride (de Kadt 1976, Leon 1987). Once craftsmaking becomes a profitable industry, its status is elevated within the community. Increased market demand then encourages intergenerational teaching about the product, and, if that product is made from native plants or nearby clays, such teaching may include information about local resources and their ecology. At best, as the authors in a recent issue of *Cultural Survival Quarterly* note (Anon. 1982), crafts markets marry the past with the present, helping to maintain cultural integrity while facilitating participation in modern-day international markets.

Innovation and Authenticity

Clearly handicrafts markets are no panacea for the troubles of the developing world. Many people assert that crafts production adulterates the longstanding standards and techniques of the culture involved. Artisans responding to tourist demand begin to create objects to please the buyer, not to fulfill a community function. This can affect surface aesthetics, as in the case of such crafts as Mexican bark paintings, which have become brighter and gaudier with increased tourist purchase (de Kadt 1976). Or, consumer demand may alter the basic design of objects, such as traditionally large water-carrying pots made tiny to accommodate the carrying capacity of tourist luggage (Graburn 1982). Even well-intentioned dealers can exert a strong influence on these pieces. As trader Edmund Carpenter (Carpenter et al. 1959) noted with regret, he and other traders working with Eskimo artisans had implicitly conveyed their own tastes, then congratulated the artisan who followed their example. Finally, a more subtle outcome of market production may be the stripping of traditional values once associated with the handcrafted object (de Kadt 1979, Schadler 1979). A mask never used in ceremony is no longer sacred; a camel bag sold as a purse has lost its original utility. For those most interested in supporting the heritage of the community involved, these changes may be most significant. In a sense, the object survives as nothing but an empty shell devoid of the custom and meaning with which it was once associated.

Conflicting perspectives on the effects of crafts promotion extend not only to the crafts object, but also to the people who produce them. As Cook (1984) describes, crafts producers suffer dual impositions from the outside: one encouraging mass-production of their traditional artistry, the other insisting that they not adulterate their pure, indigenous heritage. Artisans pursuing the market of their craft often straddle two worlds, without achieving a comfortable position in either one.

It should be noted, however, that these arguments about the demise of traditional integrity often oversimplify the histories of these crafts. Navajo rugs—a quintessential "traditional" product—only became a cultural trademark of the Navajo in the decades after the European settlement of the U.S. southwest brought that region into the international market economy (Kent 1976). Even more striking, the soapstone carvings of the Alaskan Eskimos have only been a common artform since the early 1960s (Graburn 1976). A visiting trader potentially conceived of, and definitely institutionalized this local craft so that in time it grew to become the primary source of income for many local people. From these examples, it is clear that the history of these traditions is often misunderstood, and that certain art forms may be less "sacred" than the public perceives. Ironically, though, sellers—especially commercial middlemen—may be reluctant to admit the short history of their wares, as tradition itself is a strong selling point, especially among tourist buyers.

Even if handicrafts with traditional religious or functional significance have greater consumer appeal, it is these pieces in particular whose integrity may be diminished when they become tourist items. That being the case, it may be justifiable, if not preferable, to promote crafts that have been developed specifically for market interests. Aid to Artisans (ATA) and the Asociación Mexicana de Arte y Cultura Popular (AMACUP) have sponsored a number of handicraft projects that take this approach (Morris 1992). These include the production of wooden blocks for children in Quintana Roo, and t-shirt making near El Triunfo Biosphere Reserve in Chiapas. Both products have garnered consumer interest abroad without having to prove historical connections.

In other efforts, AMACUP has encouraged the integration of traditional motifs into current crafts. Staff members of AMACUP shared their discoveries of ancient Mayan motifs with embroidery cooperatives in Quintana Roo, and used these on shirts the groups were decorating. They also researched ancient art forms that had been lost, including woven baskets and a design for a traditional men's shirt. As Morris (1992) describes it, artisans wanted to learn more about their ancestors' crafts, and warmed up to the involvement of the outsiders once their interest in traditions was expressed. Morris also asserts that these artisans were comfortable with the balance between preserving traditions and introducing innovations. Elsewhere this meeting of old and new has come in a parallel way—with traditional objects incorporating modern images such as jukeboxes, Coca-Cola insignias, and even McDonald arches (Anon. 1982, Whitten 1982).

Ultimately, concerns about cultural erosion surrounding crafts markets may be confusing cause and effect; that is, objects will not have ritual significance if the traditional beliefs have eroded anyway. More important, art by its very nature breaks with or at least replenishes tradition: it is an evolving expression of new ideas and inventions. Thus it is probably less valid, and certainly more constraining, to restrict the development of new motifs, styles, and materials than to allow them to adapt to the changing conditions of a modern world.

Who Benefits?

Handicraft production very often employs people living below the poverty line who can work out of the home with little or no investment in machinery (Leon 1987, Popelka and Littrell 1991). In rural areas, it may provide economic opportunities that help counter urban migration. Despite these strengths, certain social tensions may arise when markets are expanded. In describing the Zapotec weaving industry, anthropologist Lynn Stephen (1992) points out that women and girls who got involved in weaving still had to perform their traditional domestic chores. In this way, the work was not an alternative to unpaid labor, but an additional burden.

Another concern is that promoting handicraft industries draws people away from subsistence occupations, making them vulnerable to the unpredictable tourist and travel industries, and the changing trends and tastes of the consumer world (Graburn 1982). In addition, anthropologist Paul Henley and others argue that crafts markets can disrupt community structure by spurring individualist behavior where it did not previously exist (Milton 1992).

These concerns warrant consideration, but a host of social benefits often accompany handicraft programs, as well, and these ought not to be overlooked. Stephen (1992) describes the addition of a new school, more doctors, a yarn factory, and two pharmacies accompanying the boom of weaving sales in Teotitlán. Others have described the formation of artisan cooperatives that turn profits back into community development (Berkeley 1987, Ruddell 1987). Leon (1987) argues that the profits from handicrafts can be channeled into health care, reforestation, and other community services; that they often ensure better worker equity, marketing, and quality control; and that they set a precedent for community organization, often becoming the basis for increased political activism.

In short, any range of outcomes is possible from these artisan ventures, it is simply important to account for the specific conditions of the community and the industry.

Ecological Impacts

Of primary concern to conservation-oriented groups now involved in handicraft programs is the potential drain on natural resources used in production. In general, it is argued that creating a market price for any resource—be it a wood, a fruit, or a flower—changes the dynamics of people's relationship to that resource. In other words, cash value creates an incentive for the individual to exploit a resource that might previously have been considered more a common good.

Experience shows it is often difficult to predict the effects of crafts production on resource availability. Artisans in Kop Chen, México, for example, depleted all usable vines for their basketmaking within a short period after production began (Morris 1992). Morris also cites examples of rattan furniture-making in the Philippines and amate paper production in central México where overproduction led to depletion of local sources of the natural material. Given these potential dangers, AMACUP and ATA avoid using materials whose supplies are uncertain. Wooden blocks are made solely from scrap lumber, and other materials—such as cotton cloth and paints—are imported from central México. This approach avoids the difficult task of gauging user and resource response to industry growth.

Meanwhile, AMACUP has looked to emulate art projects with a different kind of ecological application. According to Morris, a women's, t-shirt making group outside Monteverde Biosphere Reserve in Costa Rica has become more knowledgeable about quetzals and other local birds in the process of researching designs that visiting tourists will find attractive. Following this example, AMACUP initiated its t-shirt making project outside El Triunfo Biosphere Reserve. Visiting artists

taught members of the community—many of them children—basic lessons in drawing, painting, and design; the community members then began producing t-shirts of local wildlife. Environmental education was one of the foremost goals of the program from its inception, and Morris (1992) explains that the painters have gained new interest in studying local wildlife—animals they did not pay attention to previously if they were neither food nor pests. Residents are more supportive of ecotourism in the region now, as well.

Educational benefits of handicraft markets are not limited to the artisans; oftentimes, information that accompanies products helps to educate consumers about environmental aspects of the products, as well. For example, buttons produced from the tagua palm in a Conservation International-sponsored project are sold with "hang tags" that explain how harvesting forest products can help prevent deforestation in tropical areas. A coalition of non-profit groups involved in developing such non-timber forest products has formed to evaluate claims of sustainability and local community benefits, and is now establishing more formal criteria by which their projects can be judged. Buyers of Rain Forest Crunch candy receive a similar message about the benefits of non-timber forest products. Green consumers are often eager to support products with environmental benefits; at the same time, they may gain a better understanding of the people, landscapes, and wildlife under threat throughout the world.

THE IRONWOOD STORY

For visitors to Sonora, México, ironwood carvings are nearly as prominent a part of the scene as saguaro cacti and taco stands (Fig. 1). The wooden figurines are carved by two sets of people—the Seri Indians and rural Mexicans living in Bahía Kino, Sonora—and are now sold in roadside stands, marketplaces, and craftshops from Alaska through Arizona, to central México.

The Bahía Kino region from which ironwood originates is a place of extremes. From flat brown plains

FIG. 1. Non-Seri, machine-made ironwood carvings for sale in Hermosillo, Sonora. Photograph by David Burckhalter.

forested with stark columnar cacti, the landscape shifts to a vibrant expanse of blue sea. At this confluence of habitats, the Sonoran desert boasts numerous aridland species—mesquite, paloverde, ironwood, jackrabbits, and lizards—and the Sea of Cortez supports diverse marine life—turtles, pelicans, clams and dolphins. Most of the ironwood carvings represent these varied native plants and animals—some of which are now endangered—including Gambel's quail, bighorn sheep, sea turtles, dolphins, and roadrunners, making them popular mementos for visitors from near and far.

Within the last several years, conservationists have become aware that the boom of ironwood figurines on the market has been matched by a steady decline of the tree in its native habitat. While the potential localized depletion of ironwood was recorded as early as the mid-1970s (Ryerson 1975), the severity of this depletion has only recently received more widespread attention.

Ironically, the very creatures represented by ironwood carvings are being threatened by this depletion because so many of them depend on ironwood for some aspect of their survival (Nabhan 1992). Current estimates suggest that ironwood is being rapidly depleted across an area roughly equivalent to twice the size of Massachusetts, raising serious concern about the consequences for associated life forms.

While ironwood figurines may be the most visible use of the tree to the Sonoran visitor, they by no means constitute its greatest use. Instead, it is land clearing for ejidos, or rural cooperative villages, conversion of forest to grazing land, fuelwood gathering, and the production of charcoal and oven-fired bricks that account for ironwood's primary losses.

While the ecological aspects of ironwood depletion were being addressed by the other contributors to this monograph, others of us began to set a strategy specifically focused on the ironwood crafts market. It was surmised that if all other uses of ironwood were completely limited, ironwood supplies would probably be able to meet the demands of the carving industry. Ironwood carving uses an estimated maximum of 5000 tons of ironwood each year, but different harvesting practices greatly reduce associated damages to the tree and its habitat as compared with other industries. Most notably, carvers rarely use anything but dead wood, and in most cases the wood is cut selectively. If single dead branches are cut for carvers' use, they will usually resprout, so coppicing methods can be employed for long-term use.

Furthermore, the carving industry has economic justification on its side, as it employs far more individuals than does the charcoal industry, and generates 100 times the income for the same weight of wood. These factors, combined with concern about threats to Seri culture, led us to support the ironwood crafts industry, but with a program that would accommodate cultural and ecological constraints.

Ironwood Artisans—Past and Present

The first step in designing a conservation strategy targeted at ironwood carvers was to understand the unique cultural dimensions of the industry. On the face of it, the situation seemed to be one of an indigenous population—the Seri—losing their strength on the marketplace not so much because of diminished ironwood supplies, but because of the overwhelming competition of neighboring Mexican communities. While Seri carve figurines with hand tools, Mexican carvers use electric sawing and sanding tools that enable them to increase production by as much as a factor of ten. As a result, non-Seri carvings dominate tourist stands and shops, and the price for individual carvings has dropped so much in recent years that Seri have a difficult time selling their pieces at profit. Here, as elsewhere, our understanding of the situation grew more complicated at every turn.

Concern for the plight of the Seri stems in part from their almost symbolic stature among Native Ameri-

cans, as they comprise one of the last remaining hunter-gathering societies in North America. Never numbering more than 2000 people, they are today only 600 men, women and children who have prevailed in the region for centuries through extensive knowledge of their local environment (Felger and Moser 1985; Juarez, pers. comm.). Today, most of the Seri live in one of two villages—Punta Chueca and El Desemboque—located more than an hour by unpaved road from the Mexican fishing community of Bahía Kino. Cash income is gained through fishing, harvesting jojoba, and selling crafts—primarily shell/bead/bone jewelry, baskets, and ironwood carvings (Juarez, pers. comm.). The Seri communities are neither thriving nor collapsing; but their ability to continue to make a living entirely off of wild resources and within their coastal villages has become increasingly difficult.

In delving more deeply into Seri history, we gained insights into the quality of their interaction with outside groups, and into their use of ironwood. Traditionally, the Seri occupied small seasonal camps along the Sea of Cortez coast and on the nearby island of Tiburón. Their nomadic lifestyle allowed them to track wildlife and water supplies, while reducing the chance of depletion of plant or animal resources (Felger and Moser 1985). Fishing provided the majority of their food, but the Seri used many kinds of local plants and animals for tools, clothing, toys, and other basic goods.

Despite contact with Spanish missionaries beginning in the 16th century, not to mention increasing contact with Mexican fishing and tourist communities in the 20th century, the Seri have resisted outsiders' attempts to integrate them completely into Mexican society. Christianity was embraced by some Seri families, but it did not fully supplant traditional beliefs. Attempts to make the Seri become agriculturalists failed in almost every case. On the whole, the Seri took advantage of some outside resources and the opening of outside markets, but remained relatively autonomous. Nonetheless, diseases such as tuberculosis and measles, along with sporadic warfare, took a heavy toll on Seri populations, which fell to less than 200 at one time (Felger and Moser 1985). Spanish settlement reduced Seri range and water resources, and until recently, the military has limited the use of such traditional hunting grounds as Tiburón Island.

Major changes to the Seri culture occurred in the 1950s when Mexican tourist and fishing industries expanded at Kino. At one and the same time, marine resources were drastically diminished by Mexican and Japanese exploitation, and store foods were made available. With the introduction of a cash economy, Seri entered into the local and eventually the international marketplace by selling goods they had previously only taken for personal use.

While it comes as a surprise to many, it was not until this recent decade that ironwood carving became a common Seri creation. True, ironwood carving has its origins in traditional Seri uses stemming back hundreds of years: the Seri carved the wood into harpoon shafts, boat oars, and violin bows; burned it for fuelwood; formed it into a ball for men's foot ball games; and made it into "bull-roarers" to summon supernatural powers at the end of a person's vision quest (Ryerson 1975, Felger and Moser 1985). But carving wooden figurines is, like soapstone carving of the Inuits, a decidedly recent phenomenon—both for the Seri and for the neighboring Mexican carving communities.

Seri artisan José Astorga is credited with beginning the ironwood carving industry sometime in the mid-1960s—first carving the wood into hair barrettes and paperweights, and later into three-dimensional animals, humans included. According to Ryerson (1975), a woman living in Hermosillo may have encouraged Astorga's carving inclinations and even preceded him by carving ironwood into animal-shaped doorstops. Regardless, Astorga originated the Seri ironwood carving tradition as it is known to outsiders, providing bush pilot Ike Russell with the earliest figurines now in museum collections (Felger and Moser 1985).

Spurred by interest from outsiders, especially two or three University of Arizona students, Astorga and

FIG. 2. Seri carver Armando Torres at work in Desemboque, Sonora. Photograph by David Burckhalter.

then his extended family expanded and refined their carving techniques. According to Ryerson (1975), the market had opened at a critical time: the fishing industry was near collapse and the Seri were desperately in need of new sources of income. Soon after Astorga created the first ironwood carvings, virtually every Seri household produced ironwood carvings which they sold directly to visiting tourists or to the student middlemen (Fig. 2).

The Seri were not the only inhabitants of Sonora affected by reduced fishing stocks; Mexican fishing communities also felt the change. When a Sonoran man named Aurelio Palma returned to Bahía Kino in 1972 after learning ironwood carving techniques from the Seri in Punta Chueca, he found a ready supply of would-be apprentices. A large network of carvers in Bahía Kino was soon established, one which today includes at least 50 carving cooperatives and several hundred individual

FIG. 3. Non-Seri ironwood worker in Bahía Kino, Sonora. Photograph by David Burckhalter.

carvers (Briones, pers. comm.). All told, 2000-3000 non-Seri craftsmen are now employed in the ironwood industry in at least eight Sonoran cities and two towns in Baja California.

For the Seri, ironwood carvings once constituted a huge source of income, but the involvement of carvers at Bahía Kino has reduced their market (Ryerson 1975). The Seri, who still use only hand-held tools, cannot compete with the output of machine-assisted operations of the Mexican communities. Mass production techniques enable Mexican artisans to produce 20-50 times the number of carvings a Seri can make by hand in a given week, and thus to supply markets with higher stocks at a price too low for Seri carvers to meet (Fig. 3). These advantages have led Mexican carvers to dominate the massive export market, and, in turn, for the Seri to experience a decline in annual income. At the same time, the rapid consumption of ironwood by non-Indian

Mexican carvers led to local scarcities of dead wood and rising prices, as well as greater distances travelled to obtain ironwood raw materials. The number of Seri ironwood carvers has dropped from a high of 150 during the 1970s, to less than 15 regular carvers by 1992.

Designing a Conservation Strategy

During early phases of field work in the summer of 1992, conversations with several Seri artisans led us to believe that they held little resentment about the competition from neighboring Mexican communities. We could see that although the Seris are the originators of the ironwood art form, they had only been carving little more than five years longer than Mexican craftsmen. Both are decidedly new traditions that have come to play a central role in the economies of the Sonoran communities.

But in the summer of 1993, a gathering of Seri in Bahía Kino revealed a deeper level of frustration about the status of their art, and new insights into issues of cultural claims. The Seri did express resentment about the low prices of Mexican ironwood carvings. They complained of difficulties obtaining access to ironwood, and cited recent intrusions onto their land by non-Seri ironwood cutters. And, most of all, they were dismayed by what we told them about inaccurate labelling of non-Seri carvings.

Taking advantage of collectors' penchants for "genuine Indian art," many sellers—especially in the United States—display mixed assemblages of Seri and non-Seri carvings with labels that read "made by the Seri Indians of México." Some go so far as to attach stickers with the words "Seri-made" or "Indian-made" directly onto the ironwood pieces. At a 1993 gathering, members of the Ironwood Alliance shared examples of information tags found both in México and in other countries which misrepresented the carvings and the Seri.

For those who know the carvings well, Seri and Mexican carvers have noticeably different styles. Among the basic differences are that Seri carve almost exclusively plants and animals native to their desert home. They rarely carve fish other than sharks, do not carve horses or felines, and do not carve inanimate objects. By contrast, a collection of ironwood carvings made by Mexican carvers will include a tremendous range of subjects—including marlins, unicorns, baseballs, bulls, lions, and even Tecate beer bottles. Surface workmanship also reveals basic differences: almost all of the Seri sand their pieces to a smooth surface, and do not mark the surface with anything more than an occasional eye nick. The result is a simple, elegant piece tending more towards abstraction than realism. Mexican carvers, on the other hand, strive for much more detailed, textured, and realistic figures. In addition to more morphologically-literal shapes, the pieces will often have a textured surface made to resemble feathers, fur, and turtle shell designs.

It has been noted, too, that the subtleties of Seri pieces reflect direct experience of the animal or plant; for example, a sea turtle may be carved with very large front flippers that show that it is a baby turtle, or a toad may be carved in a crouched position it only takes when threatened (Felger and Moser 1985). Also, many Seri carvings are considered to catch the "essence" of the animal—its spirit or movement—with great efficacy.

From the start, Ironwood Alliance members sought ways to clarify the distinctions between Seri and non-Seri art and to reduce illegal labelling. Educational outreach targeted at storeowners and buyers met with some success, but attempts to have artisans themselves label their carvings had simply never succeeded. After the 1993 meeting, however, we renewed efforts to regulate ironwood carvings. With the assistance of Marta Turok of AMACUP, the Ironwood Alliance has helped the Seri in efforts to obtain from the Mexican government a "denominación de origen"—certification of origination. This certification, if obtained, would not necessarily give Seri exclusive rights to carve ironwood, but it would grant them recognition as the art form's exclusive originators and would protect certain styles of carving. After all, if consumers seek the Seri product, they should be getting it, and paying the price that reflects its true cost. Otherwise, the Seri will have a difficult time making

the profits they deserve.

Of course, the carving differences are clearer and simpler on paper than they are in real life, and the lines have grown increasingly blurred. It has even been suggested that some Seri carvers may be purchasing Mexican carvings and finishing them by hand before selling them as their own.

Even harder for those of us involved with the project to sort through was an apparent shift in our dynamic with local artisans. In 1992, we had engaged not only Seri, but also an enthusiastic contingent of Mexican carvers, in our discussions and policies about ironwood. We had made it very clear that we would not, could not, make judgements about the two groups' respective rights to carve dead wood from this tree as long as all carvings were truthfully labelled. But through the unexpected events of our week-long stay in 1993, we found ourselves more ambivalent about our alliance with our Mexican carving group. While the certificates of origination would not preclude non-Seri carving, they did reflect an underlying favoring or approval of Seri, original carving. More than 80 Seri signed a petition to the Mexican government requesting stricter controls on their competitors.

We struggled with this dilemma, then resolved that our best course of action was to visit the Mexican carvers and cooperatives and update them on our work and our reasoning. Better to hear it from us than from some other source. We also came to see that the five-year difference between Seri and Mexican carving histories was more significant than we had first thought; it did, we recognized, mark the difference between creator and copier.

At this time, the certification of origination process has not been finalized, and other avenues are being investigated, such as "registro de marca colectiva" offered by SECOFI, a Mexican government agency which registers a region or trademark. In the meantime, we have renewed outreach efforts to storeowners with a mass mailing of letters and questionnaires to gauge their understanding of the cultural/ecological issues surrounding ironwood. In the meantime, we have designed new labels for the Seri to use on their carvings.

Alternative Materials

Given that ironwood is already so severely depleted and the costs of purchasing dead ironwood on permit are increasingly prohibitive, one is left to consider the option of discontinuing the carving industry entirely, or finding innovative ways to make it last. Carvers themselves expressed concern that they would soon have to shift occupations. Since shutting down the ironwood industry would probably be unfeasible, and certainly abrupt, we decided to try the second approach. Our crafts program had several components: first, to step up controls of ironwood obtained for carving purposes; next, to reduce the present and future demand for ironwood by introducing alternative carving materials; and finally, to help find markets for these newest materials.

To improve legal harvesting of ironwood, we considered developing a program to ensure that carvers obtain wood only from permitted cutters; currently, an estimated 10% of wood for the crafts industry is obtained without permit. This would avoid depletion of ironwood in endangered habitats and create an incentive for woodcutters to obtain regulated permits. We initially thought that carvers who followed this process could receive a special stamp of approval—a certification that theirs were "environmentally-safe" carvings. But in light of the speed with which broader regulation of the woodcutting industry has been enforced, our own enforcement strategy seemed less pressing, and it was never clear the stamping process would have succeeded in such a loosely-controlled industry.

More progress has been made on the second part of the program; namely, introducing alternative carving materials to Seri and Mexican carvers. The approach is not altogether novel. Since the development of the Seri ironwood carving tradition, craftsmen have experimentally carved a range of materials native to their region or introduced by visiting middlemen. These include soapstone, pipestone, osage orange, cherry wood, and a local

stone known as *barita*, or barite. When ironwood was readily obtainable and easy to sell, none of these materials gained lasting popularity among carvers. Recent scarcity, however, has led artisans, traders, and conservationists alike to renew experimentation with alternative carving materials. To date, the following materials have demonstrated the greatest potential for success:

1) Barite. This sedimentary rock is relatively soft but has a very high specific gravity. Available from local quarries, it is already carved by a few Seri into cruder forms than is ironwood. One appealing trait of barite is its color, which can range from sea-foam blue to a checkerboard of brick red and white, lending an interesting dimension to certain pieces. Early in the project, most barite carvings we saw were crude and inexpert, with the notable exception of sculptures of seals on rocks. By the summer of 1993, however, we found a number of truly outstanding barite carvings, giving us

FIG. 4. Barite carving of a porpoise. Photograph by Sara St. Antoine.

new hope of the stone's potential (Fig. 4). Barite has the important advantage of being locally available in great quantities.

2) Tagua. In recent years, Conservation International has sponsored the harvesting of this tropical palm nut in Ecuador and Colombia as an alternative to forest clearance. When carved, tagua has the color and consistency of ivory. It has been used to make jewelry, fetishes, and buttons for clothing manufacturers in the United States, and is available in bulk quantities imported from the tagua community harvesting groups.

With the help of Jim Hills, long-time trader and friend of the Seri, we introduced tagua and appropriate carving tools to several Seri craftsmen. Seri carver Nacho Barnett had great success on his first round, making small shells, pelicans, bears, and more. Following Hills' suggestion, Barnett left patches of the brown outer surface of tagua to highlight wing tips, beaks, etc. This measure not only adds an attractive texture to the carvings, but reduces the likelihood of the pieces being held up at customs because of their close resemblance to elephant ivory.

Although we also provided tagua to Mexican carvers in Bahía Kino, its small size made it difficult to carve with their large sawing and sanding tools, and they did not express interest in obtaining more samples. It remains to be seen whether Seri carvers will maintain interest in such a foreign material, but CI has continued to supply quantities of "jumbo tagua" to the Seri at no cost.

3) Alternative tropical hardwoods. An agro-forestry group known as Quintana Roo Forestry Societies and Collectives, located in this southern Mexican state, harvests a variety of tropical hardwoods. At no charge to the carvers, the group sent a batch of sample woods by train to Hermosillo, and members of our group distributed these woods to Mexican and Seri carvers. Unfortunately the first load contained flat planks unsuitable for three-dimensional pieces, but both groups were excited about the new woods and expressed interest in obtaining larger pieces of certain species.

We were pleased when the Mexican carvers' expressed concern not only about whether these woods would be as inexpensive to obtain as ironwood (factoring in travel costs), but also about the true level of "sustainability" of the agroforestry projects. In response, we are in the process of determining total costs for these woods, and México's AMACUP has agreed to assess the long-term viability of these and other alternative materials.

In 1992, we conceived of having a Bahía Kino resident serve as a liaison with agroforesters in Quintana Roo. This person would oversee shipments of hardwoods and other materials to the carvers, and perhaps help deliver the carvings to the appropriate markets. The single most important objective of this effort would be to formalize the alternative materials industry and create the necessary structure so that our intervention was no longer necessary to keep people involved. Unfortunately, the funding and hiring process for this new position have not yet been secured.

4) Clay. At the 1993 summer gathering in Bahía Kino, we enlisted the aid of sculptor John Piet to facilitate a clay sculpting workshop. Quite simply, Piet sat at a table beneath a tree and sculpted pieces of his own while making the clay available for any interested takers. There were many. In many ways, the clay corner was one of the most important parts of the gathering, as it gave everyone—especially women and children—a place to sit and watch, or to quietly create clay pieces of their own. This experience was not merely a diversion; it eased the strains between outsiders and insiders, and engaged the Seri in the process of developing a new material, rather than just delivering it to them. As it was, the Seri had presented us with small, primitive human clay figures earlier in the week, so once again they showed their own innovative capabilities. In the following weeks, clay beads appeared on many shell necklaces, hand-molded bowls and cups were created, and new animal figurines of clay were offered to visitors of Punta Chueca.

Attracting Consumer Interest

In the process of exploring alternative materials for Kino artisans to carve, we recognized that tagua, tropical hardwoods, and to some extent barite are all new enough crafts that they might not gain immediate market interest on par with current ironwood popularity. Given that carvers are likely to need rapid results to convince them of the viability of these new materials, we decided to jumpstart their market with a travelling art exhibit. All of the art traders with whom we spoke agreed that popular interest in indigenous art typically follows collectors' interests, and that a collector's interest begins in art exhibits. A well-designed art exhibit would, moreover, serve a valuable educational purpose by informing the public about the importance of ironwood to the Sonoran Desert community, and showing them how culture and conservation can intersect.

Significant progress has been made with the early phases of the art exhibit. Curators at the Heard Museum in Phoenix and the Museum of Folk Art in Santa Fe expressed interest in and support for the exhibit, and a proposal was submitted to the Smithsonian Institution Travelling Exhibit (SITES) program to help develop and schedule the program. SITES did not accept our proposal for a full exhibit, but instead included a small display on the issue in its "Two Eagles/Dos Aguilas: Wildlife on the U.S./México Borderlands" exhibit that began travelling throughout the United States in October 1993. This display is comprised of a sample "tree of life" carving and text, and will appear in major museums and other public spaces over the next three years.

To accompany such exhibits, I wrote a brochure text, which was then produced in English and Spanish by graphic designer Ramon Perez Gil, to discuss the background of the ironwood crafts industry and the cultural and ecological issues surrounding it. This brochure has also been distributed to regional crafts shops for further public education.

Generous local support for education has come through other channels, as well. Arizona artist Annie Coe agreed to do a large painting of the ironwood tree surrounded by its associated wealth of life. Proceeds from the sale of the painting will go to the ironwood project, and Coe gave us free rights to her design for use on posters and t-shirts that will accompany and help finance the exhibit. Paul Mirocha also designed another poster, "Protege El Palo Fierro—Fuente de la Vida del Desierto," which has been exhibited in more than a dozen Sonoran towns and cities.

Also, Jim Hills, director of Native and Nature—a store specializing in products that represent regional culture and ecology—devoted his entire 1992 winter catalog to the ironwood theme. In addition to running information about ironwood throughout the catalog, Hills donated 10% of the gross income from the catalog to the ironwood project. His shops will be an obvious market for future Seri products, as well.

The Ironwood Alliance has also involved a number of talented writers who have helped alert consumers to the issue through a variety of media outlets: *World Monitor, Longevity, E, Pacific Discovery, Newsweek,* and *Amicus* magazines; the bilingual *Sonoran Journal* and the *San Francisco Chronicle*, as well as Pacifica and CBS radio.

All tolled, it is hoped that these combined efforts will not only interest the general public in alternative materials products, but will engage them in the Seri ironwood story.

EVALUATION OF IMPACTS

The handicraft aspects of the ironwood conservation project have had to be reevaluated throughout the project, and even now will undoubtedly undergo changes as new information and attitudes are accounted for. Nonetheless, one can already begin to evaluate the merits of this program in the context of issues raised in the first part of this paper.

First, from a cultural standpoint, ironwood carvings do not have a sacred history which outside intervention could disrupt. From the outset, external market demand influenced the quality of Seri carvings, as well as the quantity. Responding to buyer preferences, for example, Seri carvers ceased the practice of affixing eyes to the figures, began to polish the carvings with shoe polish or waxes to increase their sheen, and carved almost exclusively figures of native wildlife. Both Seri and non-Seri carvings can be viewed as modern-day commodity items.

This bears particular relevance to the expansion into alternative carving materials which we have promoted among the ironwood carvers. Some might claim that it is unnatural and unauthentic to encourage the use of non-local materials, and perhaps it is less than desirable. On the other hand, this resource exchange across the Republic of México, and between Ecuador and México, reflects the increasingly global community of which the Seri and Mexican carvers are now part. Moreover, precedence for such an exchange extends far back in history to the early importation of beads, metals, and other materials to Native American artisans, which are now widely considered part of the authentic Native American artistic heritage. In general, both sets of carvers with whom we worked were eager to try anything new, and seemed excited about the prospects of having more available materials with which to work. One concern that did surface in our group had to do with bringing in carvings from other regions—such as Zuni fetishes and Inuit sculpture—to demonstrate the potential of alternative materials. Would this introduction lead the Seri to copy the designs themselves, rather than initiating their own "authentic" ideas? This remains one of the unresolved questions of the program.

Concerns about whether promoting ironwood crafts will draw artisans away from subsistence occupations are largely moot in the Seri case; crafts production began when subsistence activities alone could not meet their basic needs, so in a sense it was already too late to be concerned about the consequences of shifting occupations. Furthermore, the Seri have never abandoned their subsistence activities, and continue to harvest desert and marine products for their own use and for sale. In fact, CI has recently introduced mesquite grinding mills to the Seri to allow them to make more frequent use of the nutritious legume pods. Most important, the Seri industry grew from within the community, and was largely pursued by them, not thrust upon them. Similarly, the communities of Bahía Kino chose for themselves to enter the carving market when fishing began to lose its economic security.

Economically, production of figurines from ironwood and alternative materials is a low-investment effort for the Seri, requiring only a few strong knives for carving. It employs both men and women from Seri villages, although it is not clear who gains ultimate control of the income within the family unit. The greatest economic issue in terms of ironwood carvings is the dismally low prices the Seri must sell their pieces for in order to compete with the Mexican carvers. Because each piece takes so much of their time to produce, their income for labor expended is much lower than that of Mexican artisans.

Ryerson (1975) also claims that the Seri have not adapted well to the cash economy in that few of them have mastered the art of saving or forecasting times of low income flow. One potential aid to the Seri communities, then, might be to encourage the formation of artisan cooperatives—an approach that has worked well in other areas (Leon 1987). While many of the Mexican carvers of Old Kino have already formed cooperatives, it may be that Seri culture and community structure do not lend themselves to this type of organization; the only Seri crafts cooperative has been inactive for years.

Concerns about the effects of markets on the Seri people may not be as relevant as they would with a different group of people. The Seri have already participated in markets of some sort for several decades and demonstrated a keen ability to adapt outside forces to their needs, rather than the reverse. In other words, the Seri have historically demonstrated that they are both opportunistic and stubborn about retaining their cultural identity; there is little reason to think that continuing to promote the ironwood carving industry in general, or, specifically, supporting the alternative materials market, will change this pattern of behavior.

Ultimately, the most critical question of our program comes down to its environmental impacts—above all, whether ironwood supplies can be sustained. No group is immune from the proclivity to overharvest, and on some level, local supplies of ironwood <u>have</u> been diminished by carvers' harvesting. On the other hand, it is certain, as was stated earlier in this paper, that ironwood is not yet rare on the Seri reservation lands even after three decades of carving. Ironwood supplies would be in much better condition throughout its range if illegal uses of the tree by non-Indians were not occurring. Diversifying carving materials to include barite, tagua, tropical hardwoods, and clay will hopefully create a more balanced extraction scenario, in which carvers can have the same or greater output of crafts pieces without overdependence on any single resource. Should any single material come into great demand, it might incite accelerated harvesting, but hopefully this outcome could be controlled by the operations at the respective harvesting sites (Quintana Roo, Ecuador, Colombia, etc.).

Several other environmental benefits accompany the carving process, as well. One is the education of consumers who come to see the wildlife of Sonora evoked through these objects and who, if they read a brochure or attend an exhibit, might gain even greater environmental sensitivity. Already considerable media attention has focussed on the damaging aspects of mesquite charcoal production, and the false labelling of ironwood carvings—both of which have generated consumer response. The carvers themselves have also participated in a variety of forums related to their industry that have raised their understanding of ironwood's ecological importance.

Should the diversifying of carving materials and related measures fail to achieve their conservation objectives, more thought could be given to whole new crafts industries which continue to support the cultural heritage of the Seri people. Basketweaving has become increasingly profitable, with some very finely woven baskets being sold to American collectors for as much as $3000. Shell necklaces, while very cheap, are easy for the Seri to produce in large quantities, and popular among tourists.

In sum, ecological concerns abound in the ironwood example, but individuals involved in the project have demonstrated a remarkable commitment to seeing them addressed. With innovation and flexibility, it is likely that these challenges will continue to be met.

Example or Exception?

In assessing the wider applications of the ironwood project to other handicraft industries, certain unique dimensions become apparent. These include the nature of the Seri people—a group that has proven themselves adaptable to change, but also resistant to imposition. This combination of characteristics makes them an ideal group to work with in suggesting new initiatives; one senses that they will only participate in those ventures they find attractive and cannot be forced to do something they do not want to do. Another unique dimension of the project is the nature of the resource. Ironwood can be harvested without complete destruction of the tree; therefore its use has greater potential for sustainability than do many other products. This characteristic extends to some other materials used in art production, such as seeds or grasses, but not to such materials as wood products that require the whole tree, animal ivory, fur products, etc. A final unique dimension is the nature of outsiders who have worked with the Seri over the last several decades. A uniquely able group of middlemen, most of them are culturally-sensitive anthropologists first, and traders second. When researching this project, it quickly became apparent that all those who work with the Seri know each other, know the Seri well, and continue to have lasting friendships with members of the Seri community. For this reason, social and economic disruption—which might have been more pronounced with influence from less magnanimous individuals—appears to have been minimal.

Despite these unique features, the ironwood example suggests positive potential for uniting conservation and cultural aims through handicraft markets. The markets should not be developed too quickly, however, and they must stop to consider the wide-ranging positive and negative effects they might have on the local environment and its inhabitants. In general, the following guidelines are suggested:

1) those developing art markets should work directly with artisans and allow them full authority to choose the direction of their trade;

2) handicraft markets should make use of a variety of materials and, ideally, produce a variety of art pieces; that is, all eggs should not be put in one basket;

3) written materials that explain the cultural and ecological context of the items should accompany their sale. This educates the public about these issues, while increasing interest in the product, and may have greater impact than formal certification programs;

4) where possible, exhibits and other displays should be promoted to engage new collectors in the items being developed. Further thinking is needed in this area, as affecting collector interest has proven exceedingly difficult in the ironwood/alternative materials example;

5) finally, while each initiative will face its own unique complications, the involvement of conservationists, anthropologists, and local people working together best assures a successful, appropriate initiative.

CONCLUSIONS

As the ironwood case study demonstrates, the development of handicraft markets from local materials carries not only great promise, but also distinct challenges, risks, and potential problems. Averting the negative effects on both people and resources will undoubtedly be one of the primary goals of any arts initiative. To that end, conservation groups will need to share the successes and

setbacks of their projects. The story of ironwood crafts presented here represents neither the end of our own work in Sonora, nor the last word on handicraft markets; rather, it marks a starting point for ongoing discussion and essential debate.

LITERATURE CITED

Anon. 1982. Introduction. Cultural Survival Quarterly 6(4):3-6.

Berkeley, L. and C. Haddox. 1987. Tarahumara handicrafts and economic survival. Cultural Survival Quarterly 11(1):57-58.

Carpenter, E., F. Varley, and R. Flaherty. 1959. Eskimo. University of Toronto Press, Toronto.

Cook, J. 1984. Peasant economy, rural industry, and capitalist development in the Oaxaca Valley, Mexico. Journal of Peasant Studies 12: 3-39.

de Kadt, E. 1979. Arts, crafts, and cultural manifestations. Pp. 68-76. *In*: Tourism—Passport to Development? Oxford University Press, Oxford, UK.

Felger, R. S. and M.B. Moser. 1985. People of the Desert and Sea. Univ. Arizona Press, Tucson.

Graburn, N. 1976. Eskimo art: the eastern Canadian Arctic. Pp. 39-55. *In:* N. Graburn (ed), Ethnic and Tourist Arts: Cultural Expressions from the Fourth World. Univ. California Press, Berkeley.

Graburn, N. 1982. The dynamics of change in tourist arts. Cultural Survival Quarterly 6(4):7-11.

Israel, P. and M. Guerre. 1982. The Amazon in plexiglass. Cultural Survival Quarterly 6(4):15-17.

Kent, K.P. 1976. Pueblo and Navajo weaving traditions and the western world. Pp. 85-101. *In:* N. Graburn (ed), Ethnic and Tourist Arts: Cultural Expressions from the Fourth World. Univ. California Press, Berkeley.

Leon, L. 1987. Artisan development projects. Cultural Survival Quarterly 11(1):49-52.

Milton, K. 1992. Civilization and its discontents.

Natural History 1992(3):36-43.

Morris, W.F., Jr. 1992. Artisans and ecology—the first two years. Asociación Mexicana de Arte y Cultura Popular and Aid to Artisans. Unpublished project report.

Nabhan, G.P. 1992. Ironwood: Nurseries of the Sonoran Desert. Conservation International Annual Report, pp. 12-14.

Nash, J. 1991. Household production and the world debt crisis. Review of Latin American Studies 3:7-35.

Popelka, C. and M. Littrell. 1991. The influence of tourism on handcraft evolution. Annals of Tourism Research 18:392-413.

Ruddell, P. 1987. Los Pilares: Lima's handicraft cooperative. Cultural Survival Quarterly 11(1):59-60.

Ryerson, S.H. 1975. Seri ironwood carving: an economic view. Pp. 119-136. *In*: N. Graburn (ed), Ethnic and Tourist Arts: Cultural Expressions from the Fourth World. Univ. of California Press, Berkeley.

Schadler, F. 1979. African arts and crafts in a world of changing values. Pp. 146-156. *In*: E. de Kadt (ed), Tourism—Passport to Development? Oxford Univ. Press, Oxford, UK.

Stephen, L. 1992. Marketing ethnicity. Cultural Survival Quarterly 16(4):25-27.

Whitten, D. 1982. Amazonian ceramics from Ecuador: continuity and change. Cultural Survival Quarterly 6(4):24-25.

Interviews

Mark Bahti, ironwood trader and art dealer. Tucson, AZ. June 15, 1992.

Reyes Briones, Mexican ironwood carver and coop director. Bahía Kino, Sonora. June, 1992.

David Burckhalter, photographer and Seri art trader. Tucson, AZ. June 15, 1992.

Victor Juarez, office of indigenous peoples. Bahía Kino, Sonora. July 28, 1992.

Jim Hills, ironwood trader and president of Native & Nature craftshops. Tucson, AZ. June 16, 1992 and throughout the summer.

Scott Ryerson, Seri art trader and anthropologist. Tucson, AZ. June 17, 1992. Peter Welsh, Chief Curator, Heard Museum. Phoenix, AZ. July 1, 1992.

S. St. Antoine
School of Forestry and Environmental Studies
Yale University
New Haven, CT 06511 USA
present address
1421 Roxbury Road
Ann Arbor, MI 48104 USA

PLANT NAMES LIST

The following list contains species of the Sonoran Desert flora in relation to ironwood (*Olneya tesota*) canopies. This list was compiled from G.P. Nabhan's field notes from Bahía Kino, Quitovac, Organpipe, Caborca and Sonoyta (1991-1993), and from the Búrquez and Quintana, and Tewksbury and Petrovich papers in this volume. + = positively associated with *O. tesota*; * = on sites with *O. tesota*, but not yet found under its canopies, or negatively associated with it; †=exotic species.

TALL ARBORESCENTS

* *Bursera fagaroides* (H.B.K.) Engler: fragrant bursera

* *Bursera hindsiana* (Benth.) Felger: red elephant tree, copalquin, torote prieto

+ *Bursera laxiflora* S. Wats.: elephant tree, torote prieto, copal

+ *Bursera microphylla* Gray: elephant tree, torote blanco

+ *Cercidium floridum* Benth.: blue palo verde, palo verde

+ *Cercidium microphyllum* (Torr.) Rose & Johnst.: foothills palo verde, palo verde

+ *Fouquieria columnaris* (Kell.) Curran: boojum, cirio

+ *Guaiacum coulteri* Gray: guayacán

+ *Olneya tesota* Gray: ironwood, palo fierro

+ *Prosopis glandulosa* Torr.: honey mesquite, mezquite

+ *Prosopis velutina* Woot.: velvet mesquite, mezquite

LARGE SHRUBS

+ *Acacia greggii* Gray: catclaw, uña de gato

* *Acacia occidentalis* Rose: tesota

+ *Atamisquea emarginata* Miers: desert caper, palo hediondo

+ *Caesalpinia palmeri* S. Wats.: bird of paradise, piojito

+ *Calliandra californica* Benth: false mesquite, tabardillo, mesquitillo

+ *Castela peninsularis* Rose: crucifixion thorn, corona de cristo

+ *Celtis pallida* Torr.: desert hackberry, garambullo, granjeno
+ *Colubrina glabra* S. Wats: snakewood
+ *Colubrina viridis* (Jones) M.C. Johnst.: palo colorado
+ *Condalia globosa* Johnst.: bitter condalia, papache, babata
+ *Coursetia glandulosa* Gray: samota
+ *Eysenhardtia orthocarpa* (Gray) Wats.: kidneywood, palo dulce
+ *Fouquieria splendens* Engelm.: ocotillo, ocote
+ *Fouquieria macdougalli* Nash: ocotillo macho
+ *Jatropha cardiophylla* (Torr.) Muell. Arg.: limberbush, sangrengrado
+ *Jatropha cinerea* (Ort.) Muell. Arg.: limberbush, torito, lomboi
+ *Jatropha cordata* (C.G. Ortega) Muell. Arg.: limberbush, jiotillo
+ *Jatropha cuneata* Wigg. & Roll.: limberbush, sangrengrado
+ *Justicia californica* (Benth.) Daniels: honeysuckle, chuparosa
+ *Karwinskia parviflora* Rose: tullidora, palo negrito
+ *Larrea tridentata* (DC.) Coville: creosotebush, gobernadora, hediondilla
+ *Lycium andersonii* Gray: wolfberry, salicieso
+ *Lycium berlandieri* Dunal: wolfberry, barchata, hoso
+ *Lycium sp.*: wolfberry, salicieso
+ *Maytenus pyllanthoides* Benth.: mangle dulce
+ *Mimosa laxiflora* Benth.: mimosa, uña de gato
+ *Pithecellobium confine* Standley: guamuchil
+ *Randia obcordata* S. Wats.: papache borracho
+ *Sapium biloculare* (Wats.) Pax.: Mexican jumping bean, yerba-de-la-flecha
+ *Vallesia glabra* Cav.: palo verde
+ *Zizyphus obtusifolia* (Hook ex T. & G.) A. Gray: graythorn, abrojo

MEDIUM-SIZED SHRUBS

+ *Acalypha californica* Benth.: yerba del cancer
+ *Ambrosia deltoidea* (Torr.) Payne: burrobush, chamizo forrajero
+ *Ambrosia dumosa* (Gray) Payne: white bursage, chamizo
+ *Apploppaus spinulosus* (Pursh) DC.: yerba de la vibora
+ *Atriplex canescens*(Pursh.) Nutt. ssp. *linearis* Hall & Clements: wingscale, cenizo
+ *Atriplex polycarpa* (Torr.) Wats.: allscale, chamizo
+ *Berginia virgata* Harv. ex Benth. & Hook: chuparosa
+ *Brickellia coulteri* (Gray): brickellbush
+ *Croton sonorae* Torr.: rama blanca
+ *Encelia farinosa* Gray: brittlebush, incienso
+ *Hymenoclea salsola* Torr. & Gray.: burrobush, jecota
+ *Hyptis emoryi* Torr.: desert lavender, salvia

+ *Krameria erecta* Willd.: range ratany, cosahui

+ *Krameria grayi* Rose & Painter: white ratany, cosahui

+ *Krameria parviflora* Benth.: ratany, cosahui

+ *Lantana horrida* H.B.K.: lantana, moradilla

+ *Lippia palmeri* S. Wats.: oregano

+ *Melochia tomentosa* L.: palo de paloma

+ *Simmondsia chinensis* (Link.) Schneid: jojoba

+ *Solanum hindsianum* Benth.: nightshade, mariola

+ *Stegnosperma halmifolium* Benth.: amole

+ *Viscainoa geniculata* (Kell.) Greene

SMALL PERENNIALS

+ *Abutilon californicum* Benth.: Indian mallow, pelotazo

+ *Abutilon incanum* (Link.) Sweet: Indian mallow, pelotazo

+ *Ambrosia ambrosioides* (Cav.) Payne: canyon ragweed, chicura

+ *Atriplex barclayana* (Benth.) Dietr.

+ *Bebbia juncea* (Benth.) Greene: sweetbush

+ *Cardiospermum corindum* Radlk.: bolsia

+ *Cassia covesii* Gray: desert senna, dais, rosamaria

+ *Chamaesyce polycarpa* (Benth.) Millsp.: desert spurge, golondrina

+ *Commelina erecta* L.: dayflower, yerba del pollo

+ *Commicarpus scandens* (L.) Standl.: sonorita

+ *Desmanthus covillei* (Brit. & Rose) Wigg. ex Turn.

+ *Ditaxis lanceolata* (Benth.) Pax & K. Hoffm.

+ *Eriogonum trichopes* Torr.: little trumpet

+ *Eriogonum wrightii* Torr.: buckwheat

+ *Euphorbia xantii* Boiss.: spurge

+ *Fagonia californica* Benth.: fagonia

+ *Hibiscus denudatus* Benth: rock hibiscus

+ *Hoffmanseggia intricata* Brandegee: hog potato, camote de ratón

+ *Horsfordia newberryi* (S. Wats.) A. Gray: orange velvet-mallow

+ *Isocoma acradenia* (Greene) Greene: alkali goldenbush

+ *Lyrocarpa coulteri* Hooke. & Harv.: lyre fruit

+ *Phaulothamnus spinescens* Gray: putia

+ *Physalis* sp.: groundcherry, miltomate

+ *Porophyllum gracile* Benth.: yerba del venado

+ *Psorothamnus emoryi* (Gray) Rydb.: indigo bush

+ *Ruellia californica* (Rose) I.M. Johnston: yerba del toro

+ *Spharalcea ambigua* Gray: globemallow, mal de ojo

+ *Stephanomeria pauciflora* (Torr.) Nutt.
+ *Tephrosia palmeri* S. Wats.
+ *Trixis californica* Kell.: trixis

LARGE CACTI

+ *Carnegiea gigantea* (Engelm.) Brit. & Rose: saguaro, sahuaro
+ *Lophocereus schottii* (Engelm.) Brit. & Rose: senita, sina
+ *Pachycereus pringlei* (S. Wats.) Brit. & Rose: cardón, sahueso
+ *Stenocereus thurberi* (Engelm.) Buxbaum: organpipe, pitahaya dulce

MEDIUM-SIZED CACTI

+ *Ferocactus emoryi* (Engelm.) Orcutt: barrel cactus, biznaga
* *Ferocactus wislizenii* (Engelm.) Brit. & Rose: barrel cactus, bisnaga
+ *Opuntia acanthocarpa* Engelm. & Bigel.: buckhorn cholla
+ *Opuntia arbuscula* Engelm.: pencil cholla, tasajo
+ *Opuntia bigelovii* Engelm.: teddybear cholla, cholla guera
+ *Opuntia fulgida* Engelm.: jumping cholla, cholla
+ *Opuntia leptocaulis* DC.: Christmas cactus, tasajillo
+ *Opuntia tesajo* Engelm. ex Coulter: tasajo
+ *Opuntia violacea* Engelm.: purple prickly-pear, duraznilla
+ *Peniocereus greggii* (Engelm.) Brit. & Rose: queen-of-the-night, jaramatraca, zaramatraca
+ *Peniocereus striatus* (Brandegee) Buxbaum: dahlia-rooted cereus, jaramatraca, zaramatraca
* *Stenocereus alamosensis* (Coult.) Gibs. & Horak: sina

SMALL CACTI

+ *Echinocereus* spp.: fishhook cactus
+ *Echinomastus erectocentrus* (Coulter) Brit. & Rose var. *acunensis* (Marshall) Bravo: acuña cactus
+ *Mammillaria grahamii* Engelm.: pincushion, cabeza del viejo
+ *Mammillaria mainae* Brandegee: fishhook cactus
+ *Mammillaria tetrancistra* Engelm.: fishhook cactus, cabeza del viejo
+ *Mammillaria thornberi* Orcutt: Thornber's fishhook cactus, cabeza del viejo

EPIPHYTES

+ *Cuscuta* spp.: dodder, cuscuta
+ *Phorodendron californicum* Nutt.: mistletoe, toji
+ *Struthanthus palmeri* (Presl.) Standley

VINES

+ *Apondanthera undulata* Gray: melón loco

+ *Aristolochia watsonii* Woot. & Standl.: Indian root, yerba del indio

+ *Ibervillea sonorae* Greene: cowpie plant

+ *Jacquemontia abutiloides* Benth.

+ *Janusia californica* Benth.: fermina

+ *Janusia linearis* Gray: fermina

+ *Mascagnia macroptera* (Ses. & Moc.) Nieden: gallinita

+ *Matelea cordifolia* (Gray) Woods.

+ *Merremia palmeri* (S. Wats.) Hallier

+ *Nissolia schottii* (Torr.) A. Gray

+ *Passiflora foetida* L.: passionflower, corona de cristo

+ *Phaseolus filiformis* Benth.: mitten-leaf bean, frijolillo

+ *Sarcostemma cynanchoides* Decne.: climbing milkweed, huirote

+ *Tumamoca macdougallii* Rose: camote de jabali

GRASSES

+ *Aristida ternipes* Cav.: spidergrass, zacate araña

* *Cathestecum erectum* Vasey & Hack.

+ *Cenchrus ciliarus* (L.)[†]: buffel grass, zacate del buffel

+ *Muhlenbergia microsperma* (D.C.) Kunth.: littleseed muhly, zacate de toro

+ *Muhlenbergia porteri* Scribn.: bush muhly, zacate aparejo

+ *Setaria macrostachya* H.B.K.[†]: plains bristlegrass, zacate temprananero

+ *Schismus barbatus* (L.) Thell.[†]: Mediterranean grass

EPHEMERALS

+ *Camissonia claviformis* (Torr. & Frem.) Raven[†]: evening primrose

+ *Chaenactis stevioides* Hook. & Arn.: desert pincushion

+ *Chenopodium murale* L.[†]: goosefoot, chual

+ *Chorizanthe* sp.: spineflower, tirebiter

+ *Conzya coulteri* A. Gray: horseweed, cola de caballo

+ *Cryptantha angustifolia* (Torr.) Greene: desert cryptantha, peluda

+ *Daucus pusillus* Michx.[†]: carrot, zanahoria

+ *Descurainia pinnata* (Walt.) Britt.: tansy mustard, pamita

+ *Euphorbia polycarpa* Benth.: spurge, golondrina

+ *Galium stellatum* Kell.: desert bedstraw

+ *Herissantha crispa* (L.) Brizicky

+ *Lepidium lasiocarpum* Nutt.: sand peppergrass, chucharita

+ *Lepidium perfoliatum* L.: shield grass, cucharita

+ *Lupinus arizonicus* Wats.: Arizona lupine, lupino
+ *Machaeranthera coulteri* (Gray) Turner & Horne: spiny aster
+ *Marina parryi* (Torr. & Gray) Barneby
+ *Melochia tomentosa* L.: dove plant, yerba de paloma
+ *Mentzelia adherens* Benth.: blazing star, pegapega
+ *Nama hispidum* Gray: waterleaf, flor morada
+ *Pectis papposa* Harv. & Gray: chinchweed, manzanilla de coyote
+ *Phacelia ambigua* M.E. Jones: desert heliotrope, tomasita
+ *Plantago insularis* Eastwood: Indian wheat, pastora
+ *Plantago purshii* R. & S.: plantain, pastora
+ *Salsola australis* R. Br.[†]: tumbleweed, Russian thistle, chamizo
+ *Solanum eleagnifolium* Cav.[†]: silver nightshade, trompillo
+ *Thelypodium* sp.
+ *Thymophylla concinna* (A. Gray) Strother: dogweed, manzanilla de coyote